The
Eight
Blessings

Rediscovering the Beatitudes

SH⋯⋯RD

ABIN⋯ ⋯IVILLE

THE EIGHT BLESSINGS
REDISCOVERING THE BEATITUDES

Copyright © 2007 by Abingdon Press

This book is printed on acid-free paper.

Library of Congress Cataloging-in-Publication Data

Stanford, Shane, 1970-
    The eight blessings : rediscovering the Beatitudes / Shane Stanford.
       p. cm.
    ISBN 978-0-687-64224-3 (pbk. : alk. paper)
    1. Beatitudes.   I. Title.

    BT382.S752 2007
    241.5'3—dc22

                                                                            2006101289

07 08 09 10 11 12 13 14 15 16—10 9 8 7 6 5 4 3 2 1

MANUFACTURED IN THE UNITED STATES OF AMERICA

For my grandmother, Dorothy,
who reminded me of why we run the race of faith

For my heroes, Jennifer and Lonny,
who show me how to run even when our bodies can't

And for my mom, June,
who has cheered and consoled me every step along the way.

One day we will kick off our shoes and run together.
Thank you for blessing me so.

CONTENTS

The Eighth Blessing: The Tension of Choice
Blessed are those who are persecuted for righteousness' sake,

SECTION THREE

ACKNOWLEDGMENTS

Of all that I write, these words are the most difficult. So many people have supported and encouraged me during this process that to recognize all of them would take innumerable words on countless pages. Thus, to everyone who has guided me with thoughts and prayers, I offer a heartfelt "thank you."

The following is a list of the individuals who remain at the center of just about everything I am and all that I do. They are the "cheering squad," yes, but also my "balance" when life gets out of control. If it weren't for these folks, none of this would be possible.

And so, from the bottom of my heart, because of you, I am, indeed, blessed!

To my editor, Pamela Dilmore, for making this process much easier than it should have been.

To Ron Kidd, and everyone at Abingdon Press, for being convinced that what I had to say truly meant something.

To the "group," Ronnie, Grif, Jimmy, and Robert, for keeping me focused on the really important issues.

To my friends and colleagues at Main Street, The Hour, and the annual conference, for your support and patience.

To Jeff, Lisa, and Jenn for your unwavering prayers.

To Jill Tryner, for her gifted organization and support.

To Patty and Nanny, for always believing in the "dream" even when I didn't.

To Mom, Buford, and Whitney, for being my biggest fans even when I didn't deserve it.

To Sarai Grace, Juli Anna, and Emma Leigh, for being my reason that each day, regardless of its challenges, remains the sweetest of blessings.

To Pokey, for being my friend, my partner, and my heart. I'll never forget 2-27. I love you.

And to Jesus, my dearest friend, for continuing to whisper the words although the vessel is often cracked and broken.

The Eighth Blessings
Rediscovering the Values of Jesus

What if you could look into the soul of Jesus and see his innermost thoughts on life? What if the general nature of all that Jesus taught could be summarized in a few paragraphs? What if the key to understanding Jesus' final words on earth rest in watching the words he used from the beginning? The Beatitudes are more than just poetic verse used to begin the Sermon on the Mount; they are the essence of Jesus' message from beginning to end. These simple and familiar words establish the overall tone of Jesus' teaching ministry and provide an intimate look at his deepest held values.

According to Matthew's Gospel, prior to the Sermon on the Mount, "Jesus went throughout Galilee, teaching in their synagogues and proclaiming the good news of the kingdom and curing every disease and every sickness among the people. So his fame spread throughout all Syria" (Matthew 4:23-24). In the Beatitudes, Jesus presents basic principles that set the stage for a deep consideration of real fellowship with God and one another. He also connects ancient and contemporary issues by echoing the Law and Prophets in every verse. The Beatitudes reveal the wholeness of Scripture and faith and, according to Jesus, serve as the building blocks for authentic spiritual relationship. *The Eight Blessings* provides a revealing look at what Jesus believed as he began his ministry on earth. Jesus' humanity forms around these truths. To hear him speak these words was to know his heart. Thus, the Beatitudes echoed throughout his ministry, and they established a God-given view of the world through the eyes of Jesus.

The Eight Blessings addresses the *simple, yet powerful, truths* of the Beatitudes as a means not only for developing our spiritual nature, but also for building true community within the scope of God's original intentions for a meaningful life. In fact, through the Beatitudes (which literally mean blessings), Jesus gives us a new definition of significance by poetically leading us to reflect on the deeper meaning of life, relationship with God, and the interconnections we have with each other. Jesus never intended the Beatitudes to serve only as road markers of lives lived well. He meant them to serve as vehicles by which to experience such a life. They are pragmatic, powerful lessons wrapped in simple words, but derived, no less, from the heart of the Son of God.

With all of the talk about values in our society, one might consider another book on the topic foolish. You cannot walk through a bookstore or pass a checkout counter without seeing a work with the latest form of *driven* or *centered* in the title. But, the values described in the following pages belong to all of us. They come from the heart of One whose life and ministry speak to our souls, relationships, actions, fears, and prejudices, for the Beatitudes address each of these and more. These values transcend the traditional how-to language of our culture. They are simple principles that yield amazing results when practiced faithfully because they are God's principles. Certainly, they address our practical needs and struggles, but they are ancient truths that transform our personal values, remove the walls we build between one another, and dismantle the façades of the many false gods we worship.

In this book, I tell stories about people and situations in order to help you make connections between the Beatitudes and contemporary life. All of the stories I tell are real in the sense that they are based upon people and situations I have encountered in my life and ministry. Some are compilations made to illustrate a particular theme. In some cases, the names and situations have been changed to honor the privacy of the persons involved.

On a more personal note, it is always humbling to approach scripture, especially when you are charged with unveiling the depth and wonder of all it has to offer. I have felt this for years every time I develop a sermon or Bible study. To do so in preparation of a book is equally, if not more, terrifying. I never claim to be a Bible scholar. Having known and been trained by some of the world's foremost experts of Scripture, for me to assume such a role would be both inappropriate and unbeneficial. Thus, *The Eight Blessings* are not meant as biblical commentary but rather as roadmarkers for the journey. My purpose in writing this book was to share my own discovery of the Beatitudes as well as gift the reader with their hope and practical meaning for life. Therefore, the core of this book rests around your reading of the Beatitudes, your assimilation of their basic, simple premises and the inclusion of your narrative with the illustrations provided.

Ultimately, *The Eight Blessings* are about Jesus in the midst of us— all of us. However, to read Scripture, we need frameworks for understanding the context, language, and meaning. Early on, I settled on two primary sources for such, William Barclay's *New Daily Study Bible* commentary and *The Interpreter's Bible* commentary series. Both works are exceptional in offering sound guidance for understanding Scripture, but also with language and exegesis that allows for the broadest of comprehension. To that end, I encourage any student of the Beatitudes to use these, or other commentaries, to delve deeper and realize the various nuances each blessing has to offer, for as much as we cover in this work, there remains infinite possibilities left to discover.

The Eight Blessings is divided into three sections. Section 1 opens with a personal, vivid recollection of my reawakening to the Beatitudes, experienced through the illness and death of my grandmother. It also describes the setting, people, and perception surrounding the scene from Matthew, and in narrative form asks you to sit at the feet of Jesus and ponder several questions: What has become of the world? Why does religion seem so out of step with daily life? Why do Jesus' simple words captivate our souls?

Section 2 addresses the Blessings themselves. In each, Jesus provides a foundation for developing the spiritually formed and significant life. For each chapter, this section uses a four-pronged approach. First, an illustration from Jesus' ministry serves as a backdrop for the lesson. Second, the lesson outlines the theme of each blessing along with its benefit. Third, illustrations highlight the subtle nuances of its relationship to our contemporary spiritual existence. And, fourth, a modern application suggests how this ancient blessing can transform our contemporary lives.

Section 3 asks the question, "Are we truly prepared for what real blessing by God means?" The nature of *makarios* (happiness) as a form of unspeakable joy that transforms our lives informs not only our spiritual existence but our daily walks as well. Knowing the power and potential of what the Eight Blessings mean is one thing; fully participating in their life-changing effect is something entirely different.

Without question, *The Eight Blessings* is decidedly Christian and spiritual. But, it is written for the believer or skeptic alike who will recognize the language of confusion, questions, and wonder. And, the book takes you on a spiritual journey through common bonds such as childhood, friendships, experiences, fears, and dreams. In the end, it provides a hopeful word of life and the possibilities of Christ's simple blessings. My hope is that you, the reader, will not look at the Beatitudes or the Sermon on the Mount the same way again and that you will be blessed!

SECTION ONE

DISCOVERY IN A FAMILIAR PLACE

I stood by the coffin and stared at the hole that would become her grave. In less than three months, the cancer ravaged her body. Although past eighty years old, she had been in relatively good health, but as often happens, the onset of the disease overwhelmed her body's defenses. As many funerals as I have been a part of over my ministry, I never remember being the last one at the grave, but as I looked around, I noticed that everyone except my wife had returned to the cars. However, this funeral was different; this grave was for my grandmother. And as I stood at the grave, I remembered the previous days and the circumstances that would alter my spiritual landscape forever.

When children and grandchildren grow up, spending time with loved ones often becomes increasingly rare. It took my grandmother's illness for me to slow my busy schedule and make an effort to visit her. By the time of her diagnosis, the cancer had spread to her stomach and pancreas, and there was little for doctors to do except, possibly, provide a few weeks or months through treatment that could be excruciating. Instead, she chose to live her last weeks in the comfort of her home, cared for by hospice nurses and surrounded by friends and loved ones.

Her home was the family home. Built in the 1920s by her in-laws, it served as a gathering place for my mother's family. It was a simple house, covered with a tin roof that provided a magical melody during rainy days. On the back of the house sat its focal point, a rustic porch complete with hand-carved swings and filled with every houseplant imaginable. My grandmother loved this porch because here she coexisted with the three things that mattered most to her: children, gardening, and God.

To my grandmother the porch was a sanctuary where things made sense. During her final days, we gathered around my grandmother on that porch to soak up each laugh and stolen moment. The children played on the swing as she watched every movement. She talked about this flower or that one, about how I should take part of it and try to root it. My grandmother knew that I couldn't grow things, but she found joy in urging me to try. And, we spent time on that porch, praying, reading Scripture, and talking about God.

Oh, how she loved God! My grandmother talked about God as a person talks about a friend. Her words were personal and intimate. She believed with all her might that faith solved every problem. No disease thwarted her hope. "And so whether I live or die...," she began. I knew the rest of Paul's words, "...for to me to live is Christ, and to die is gain" (Philippians 1:21 KJV). Although she didn't seem bothered by the prospect of what this might actually mean, I did. Maybe it was my guilt at having allowed other things to keep me from spending time with her. Maybe it was the natural reaction of all grandchildren. Maybe I just didn't understand why God allowed such wonderful saints to suffer. Regardless, just as my grandmother understood my ineptness at growing plants, she understood my confusion with her final, difficult days, and she ministered *to me* as she was dying.

I was not prepared when the Beatitudes suddenly appeared as a critical part of my devotional life. Having paid little more than an obligatory homage to them in various sermons and Bible studies, I did not find them to be enthralling. *Cursory opening words for Jesus' finest sermon,* I thought. But my grandmother loved them. In fact, every time we met, she talked about them with fond expression and description. I discovered that she learned the Beatitudes as a child in Sunday school. Like the Lord's Prayer and the Twenty-third Psalm, they served as a foundation for my grandmother's faith. She didn't just recite them from memory. She carried them about in her words as though they were precious jewels. "You can't know real joy until you are willing to experience real sacrifice," she said, hinting at the second beatitude. "It makes no difference how much you say you love someone if you are not willing to stand up for what is right," referring to the fourth. "Don't tell me you love God until you are willing to die serving Him," bluntly describing the final one. And every time she referred to the Beatitudes, she shared a new word of wisdom.

However, near the end, words became difficult for her. She drifted in and out of consciousness, but each time I bent to hug her before I left, she whispered in my ear, "Remember, you are blessed." It did not occur to me until much later that the word *beatitude* comes from the Latin for blessing.

The last visit rings especially in my memory. She was disoriented and nauseated as the disease and side effects of the pain medicine took a toll.

She had difficulty separating fantasy from reality; oftentimes her thoughts and comments reflected a type of emotional puzzle—some pieces were in place while others were missing. But, she still commanded the room as she had so many times before. She asked me to help her to the porch. "Put my shoes on. I want to run in the grass," she said. Her sister looked at her and said, "Dorothy, you know you can't run anymore." She turned to me and smiled, saying, "I am ready to run again. Let's do that when you come back." I agreed, and for the next moments, I held her hand as we simply rocked in the porch swing in silence.

As I helped her back to her bed, she pulled me close and once again whispered, "Remember, you are blessed." This time, I whispered back, "So are you, Mamaw. So are you." But looking at the makeshift hospital room complete with medicine bottles, potty seat, and adjustable bed, I was not sure how.

Every August for several years, my wife and I have taken a trip to the small, picturesque town of Fairhope, Alabama, to celebrate our anniversary. Fairhope sits on the eastern shore of Mobile Bay, and is the place of some of the most beautiful sunsets anyone could ever see. Here, my wife and I relax with our favorite pursuits. My wife loves the pool and lots of sun. I love a good book and an occasional round of golf. My grandmother seemed to get better during this time although we were not sure why. But because she seemed to rally a bit, my wife and I decided to take our annual trip, if only for a few days.

During this trip, a friend recommended a much acclaimed memoir by renowned author Annie Dillard titled *Pilgrim at Tinker Creek*. It is the story of Dillard's reflective journey in a time of personal crisis. I was captivated by the second chapter, "Seeing," in which she struggled with unrealized opportunities for meaning. In one section, Dillard talks about planting pennies on her path home when she was a child. Each day she used those marked pennies as a means of excitement and prescribed discovery. Over time, she forgot about the pennies previously placed around her, but just when she needed it, she discovered one planted nearby and ran to pick it up. My favorite quote from the book reads: "If you cultivate a healthy poverty and simplicity, so that finding a penny will literally make your day, then, since the world is in fact planted in pennies, you have with your poverty bought a lifetime of days."[1]

The Eight Blessings

The morning we were to leave from our short vacation, the phone rang. It was my stepfather calling to inform us that my grandmother had passed away during the night. As we hurriedly gathered our belongings, I could not help thinking of Dillard's quote, especially in relation to my grandmother. Her life reminded me of one who treasured the pennies planted in her path. From experiencing a difficult childhood to enduring an abusive marriage to being a young widow with four children, she lived a remarkable life of perseverance. And even as cancer ate away at her, she cultivated adversity into prosperity by watching for those simple blessings around her and by not allowing her circumstance to cloud her joy. I knew of no one who had bought a lifetime of such meaningful days with such frugal fare. My grandmother understood the value of each day and lived to make the most of it.

We finished packing and began loading the bellman's cart when I noticed my devotional guide and Bible sitting on the corner of the small desk in our room. The morning's circumstances prevented my normal devotional time. Actually, I didn't feel very spiritual. My wife, who could see my need to be with my family but also the incredible sense of disruption in my soul, suggested that we read the devotion and pray before leaving. As she found the devotion for the day, she smiled. The text for the morning's devotion was Matthew 5:1-12, the Beatitudes.

As I remembered my conversations with my grandmother, I recalled her sense of hope that God would heal her body, and I saw the look on her face when she realized that such healing would not take place in this lifetime. I watched my mother's mixed tears and laughter as she sat between her mother, who was dying, and her granddaughter, who was making funny faces to relieve the tension in the room. I felt my grandmother's hand holding mine in those final moments as she sat on the porch watching the world slip away. I heard my grandmother whisper time and again in my ear, "Remember, you are blessed." And, I wondered if I would be able, someday, to whisper such words of hope when my life finished its race. But, such ends do come. And, so, my wife and I packed our belongings and made our way home to say goodbye to one of God's dearest saints, and one of mine.

Just then, a breeze blew against the funeral home tent where, moments before, loved ones and friends had gathered to pay their respects. Several flowers turned over, and I was shaken from my daydream. As I looked at those empty chairs, the strangest feeling came over me, and I realized that what my grandmother promised was true. I am blessed. Blessed by the joy of knowing such a beautiful person. Blessed by a family with enough love to mourn honestly and laugh faithfully at the passing of a loved one. Blessed because in the loss of someone so dear, I was reminded of the simple ways that our lives matter one to another and of the insignificant ways we often miss its meaning. But I know that blessing does not happen without some consequence, without some struggle that leaves us with soul work if we are to truly understand and apply the nature of such a gift.

Over the next weeks following the funeral, I finished Annie Dillard's book, but no part of it stood out beyond that quotation on page 17. There was something almost prophetic in its verse and pragmatic in its intention. And, in some subconscious, makeshift memorial, I printed out the Beatitudes in just about every translation possible. I pinned them to my wall, read them daily, and used them as encouragement to reflect on my life and what really matters to me.

It was also during those days, as the Beatitudes hung nearby on my wall, that several major changes took place in my life. I took a new position away from the church I founded and led for nearly nine years, and I finished work on a manuscript titled *The Seven Next Words of Christ*. However, for every Next Word I studied and about which I wrote, I couldn't help thinking of those other words of Christ, proclaimed softly and almost incidentally on that mountainside, words that spoke to me now from just feet away. I pondered, "Did anyone around Jesus fully understand where these words would lead, what they might ultimately require?" I sensed that these questions were for me as well. I understood by watching and meditating on the Beatitudes the unique perspective and connection they had for my life. For none of us can truly appreciate, explain, or predefine our journey. All we can do is be aware of the simple gifts in our path each day and consider ourselves blessed. I could still hear my grandmother's words ringing around me. And, day after day I sat at my desk, suspicious that these words pinned to my wall would one day require their full due.

The Eight Blessings

No Ordinary Sermon

It was refreshing to see the crowds gather, to know there were so many eager to hear about hope instead of despair, peace instead of insurrection. Jesus learned the basic principles and power of the law from an early age. A good Jew and an incredible student of wise teachers, Jesus realized that God's law was built upon the dynamics of true relationship with God and with each other. Jesus understood that the law fostered personal fulfillment, not related to self-centered desires, but an empowered, honorable growth that benefited the person and the community. But to Jesus, the art of moral teaching was only the beginning of the law's real power for humanity. The most influential impact of the law rested upon how the law was lived out faithfully in grace among the believers.

Jesus took a seat and began speaking. This provided more than a comfortable posture from which to teach. To the Jew, this symbolized a marked connection as far back as Moses and an understanding that what was about to be shared was important. The nature of rabbinic teaching used body language and setting as much as words in order to communicate meaning. Jesus set the stage by posturing himself as one who had authority and by providing a scene by which everyone watching knew the importance of the moment.

The phrasing in the original Greek of the first verse suggested a personal connection between the message and the messenger. Jesus did not just plan to teach the bridge between the law of the prophets and this new grace offered by God, but to embody it. These were personal words spoken from Jesus' soul and heart. He intended for the disciples to recognize them as values that formed and shaped their ministry. Jesus intended for this to be one of many times that the disciples heard, pondered, and struggled with these core beliefs.[2]

Therefore, the first words of Jesus' Sermon on the Mount did more than serve as a good opening paragraph; they provided the comprehensive tone for Jesus' teachings. I imagine the scene as recorded in Matthew's Gospel. As Jesus looked out to the crowd behind the disciples, he was aware of its varied makeup—old and young, male and female, devout and skeptic, establishment and marginalized. His presence and teachings spoke beyond these categories to the heart of real-life conditions and pro-

vided a familiar word from the God too often forgotten in their generation. Jesus knew the power of simple, basic truths for a thirsty listener.
And so, he began by uttering the words, "Blessed are the poor in spirit"
(Matthew 5:3). Even the most resistant ear perked up. The disciples sat
and listened, and Jesus' sermon echoed beyond from one soul to another.

Ultimately, though, these words revealed more about Jesus than any
principle or letter of the law. For if one listened carefully, one discovered
the Beatitudes were, for lack of a better and less clichéd phrase, the core
values of Jesus. Jesus did not just preach or teach, but shared from his
own soul the nature of life and creation, an intimate work in which he
participated (see John 1). The teachings were what he knew from the
beginning; what he himself heard from the wise religious counsel he
sought; what he prayed and watched for as his time of ministry drew
close; and what he himself followed from Nazareth to the Jordan and
beyond. These teachings echoed a wisdom that transcended time and
space. Long forgotten as mere whispers of the prophets, the Beatitudes
were a clarion call of Jesus' ministry.

The blessings of Jesus do not simply rehash Hebrew teachings. They
are more than a poetic beginning to a world-class sermon. And they are
not mere symbols or rules for how we should live and act with God and
each other. They are not even a picture of what is to come, though much
of what Jesus says foreshadows better times, places, and relationships.
No, the blessings of Jesus give us a glimpse of how God's creation is
meant to be, how God intended it in the beginning. They speak of life
lived according to the ways of God's kingdom. The blessings are not simply a how-to guide for spiritual development; they are spirituality in its
truest and most genuine form.

Consider what Jesus said in these teachings. God blesses those who
realize their need for God: those who mourn, who are gentle and lowly,
who are hungry and thirsty for justice, who are merciful, whose hearts
are pure, who work for peace, who are persecuted because they live for
God. I challenge you to find a situation, encounter, parable, or miracle of
Jesus through the Gospels that does not correspond to these blessings.

And more startling, as you review the final words of Jesus on the cross
and his encounters following the Resurrection, you will see a profound
correlation. These early words of Jesus' ministry align with his final

words—speaking of hope, perseverance, love, mercy, forgiveness, and a genuine connection to God.

One cynic points out that my theory has a flaw. The *last words* and *next words* of Jesus have seven corresponding encounters, but there are *eight blessings*. My response is simple—the eighth blessing concerns persecution and how the joy of choosing God conquers the suffering of this world. Through the cross and the empty tomb, Jesus physically lived out this last beatitude and, thus, literally exemplified the nature of the eighth blessing.

To live the first seven beatitudes faithfully, we must be willing to embody the eighth in magnificent, carnal, personal terms. No saint or savior is exempt. For my grandmother to know a blessed life, she had to be willing to see the underbelly of suffering, loss, and pain. For the apostle Paul to see the unbelievable sufficiency of God's grace, he abided the thorn in the flesh. For Peter to know the unrelenting nature of Jesus' forgiveness and renewal, he endured his own fragile fears—even his denial of his friend and teacher. The Son of God suffered a humble criminal's death on a cross to redeem and restore the world.

How Does This Man Know Me?

In a world desperate for meaning and answers, Jesus offered eight simple blessings. In the process, he made himself vulnerable by sharing the values that shaped his own soul. He showed us that God deeply cares about how we act and rest in these values. Truth be told, we forget the impact of the eight blessings of Jesus' Sermon on the Mount not because they fade in and out of style, but because following them means living a transformed life. Pin the Beatitudes to *your* wall for a year and see what I mean! They affect your every move, decision, joy, sorrow, success, and failure. My grandmother was right. I am blessed! But not because every want or need is met, but because God provides the truth for life. As I take hold of God's truth, I become free. So will you.

The Beatitudes challenge the horror of our common captivity to such ills as self-sufficiency, hatred, immorality, injustice, and idolatry. They sing a new song of freedom that all can understand. In the first words of Matthew 5, Jesus offers his values and invites all human beings to live them. Of course, we Christians believe Jesus to be more than a teacher, but practicing the Beatitudes he taught makes a difference in our world whether we have faith or not. No front page headline can escape the intent of one of Jesus' blessings. And, thus, the Beatitudes of Jesus speak with power to the heart of such issues as poverty, racial injustice, religious fanaticism, familial commitment, and war, and they speak to our hearts as well.

Yes, in Matthew's Gospel, the Beatitudes mark the beginning of Jesus' ministry, but they also unveil a long awaited bridge between the hope of the ancient teachings and the promise of what God has yet to reveal. To the trained theologian, the question might be, "How could something so fresh come from something so familiar?" But to the common listener, whose life ebbs and flows day to day apart from the ponderings of philosophy and religion, the question rests even deeper: "How does this man know even me?"

One Final Glimpse

And so, as Jesus sat with his disciples, maybe once again he looked over them for a moment to catch a glimpse of the gathering crowd. Maybe, through the distance, he caught a glimpse of Calvary at this point, his humanity wondering how, with so many gathered, so few would remain in those final hours. Why would it be so hard for them? They seemed willing, but he knew the storm in their souls.

Thirty years. This moment had been in the making for thirty years. Perhaps he was recalling the stories of Bethlehem, his baptism in the Jordan, his encounter with the adversary in the wilderness, or the sermons echoing the pleas of John—"Turn from your sins and turn to God because the kingdom of heaven is near!" (see Matthew 3:2). But his reflection finished, he turned his attention to his waiting disciples and to those who had gathered to hear him speak. Clearing his voice, and with a sense of expectation of what the moment meant, Jesus began, "You are blessed...."

Notes

1. Annie Dillard, *Pilgrim at Tinker Creek* (New York: HarperCollins, 1998).

2. *Interpreter's Commentary*, vol. 7 (Nashville: Abingdon Press, 1951), 279.

The First Blessing
Having Nothing, Possessing Everything

Blessed are the poor in spirit, for theirs is the kingdom of heaven.
—*Matthew 5:3*

If you cultivate a healthy poverty and simplicity, so that finding a penny will literally make your day, then, since the world is in fact planted in pennies, you have with your poverty bought a lifetime of days.
—*Annie Dillard*[1]

Jennifer

It was her first paycheck ever, and she was giddy with excitement. In fact, I had never seen her so happy. As she waved the paper in front of me, I could tell this was no ordinary day. She kept motioning to it, and eventually, I saw the stub—her name printed on the front. "Are you going to take me to dinner?" I asked. She smiled and nodded. I continued, "Well, you tell your mom to make a date and we will celebrate." Jennifer walked toward her mom, and having heard our conversation, her mother confirmed that we would set a dinner date to celebrate Jennifer's big day. Never mind that the check was only $1.78. To Jennifer, it seemed like a million dollars.

I had met Jennifer seven years earlier when she and her family arrived at the local community center for one of the first worship services of our new congregation. Growing up Catholic, Jennifer and her family were members of a sister parish in the neighboring town but had been looking for a church closer to home. When friends mentioned to her father about our infant congregation, the family decided to visit. For all of us, it was *friendship* at first sight. They joined our church in a matter of weeks.

For years now, I have shared that story and how Jennifer and her family profoundly affected my life. In spite of the many struggles I face, it wasn't until I met Jennifer that I became truly aware of God's unbelievable, yet abundant grace. Jennifer sees the world differently from most of us. She is not self-centered. She finds joy in simple things. She loves hearts, stuffed animals, and an afternoon swim. Jennifer accepts everyone, and, even if you don't want or like it, she hugs you, forcing you to drop your protective coat and bask in the precious vulnerability that is real life. Jennifer is a champion for authentic relationships, fragility, and expectation, and she never apologizes for being so.

To say that Jennifer makes an impression is an understatement. From the moment she enters a room, she receives attention because of her electric smile and engaging personality. But there are other noticeable traits about Jennifer, for she also has cerebral palsy, a condition created from a disrupted umbilical cord at birth. She is nonverbal, and although she can walk, she has pronounced mobility issues. For many in the room, Jennifer's presence is very difficult. A sense of awkwardness and silent pity fill many as they struggle to find the words to explain or excuse their discomfort.

However, people's reactions do not concern Jennifer. Although she is a young woman now, her demeanor and interaction remind you of a small child. She approaches others with a deep innocence, as though every person she meets is a unique gift from God. In spite of a person's awkwardness or difficulty in dealing with her condition, Jennifer shows none of that awkwardness in return. Actually, moments after meeting her, Jennifer causes even the most caustic person to feel at ease, not only with Jennifer but, as many have told me later, with themselves as well.

As I stated earlier, Jennifer finds joy in simple things and, in the process, helps others to experience them as well. This is why a simple paycheck instilled such a sense of excitement and pride in her. No matter the amount of the paycheck, it was hers and that was enough.

Jennifer teaches us lessons about self-perception that many find impossible to learn. She simply meets people where they are and finds the best in all situations. When Jennifer looks at her world, she does not see limitations or the usual inhibitions that keep us from one another or God, and she does not form defenses that keep her invulnerable to those around her. On the contrary, Jennifer uses each day as an opportunity for discovery; as an occasion to find a new treasure along her path. She is content with what she has and is convinced that what she has is exactly what she needs.

No Help but God

A therapist friend of mine uses a phrase to describe the condition she sees in many couples who are unable to get at the real issues of their life together. She calls it "living from the outside in." The premise describes people who consume themselves with a reactionary life—constantly held hostage by the expectations and standards of others. Instead of establishing their own set of core values, their identities are swept up in people around them. Over time, they masquerade as high functioning individuals, but with very little truth at their core. Usually, one of life's storms disrupts their façade, and their internal structure cannot support the lie.

Just as destructive are those who choose to live totally from the "inside out." As my same therapist friend insists, these individuals consume themselves with personal issues to such a degree that they sacrifice the necessity and possibilities of community. This life, increasingly demonstrated by our culture, demands complete attention and repeated stimulation, leading to disappointment as well as bad life choices dominated by the demands of self-gratification.

In light of these competing struggles, how then does one find real meaning and direction for addressing life's many twists and turns? Jesus confronts this question with the first words of the Sermon on the Mount.

The first blessing reads, "Blessed are the poor in spirit, for theirs is the kingdom of heaven" (Matthew 5:3). For many, the first reading leads those in our modern culture to view Jesus' point as referring to mere *humility*—popularly expressed as a personal spiritual state dripping in self-denial but void of real sacrifice. However, humility is just the tip of the iceberg.

There are two words for "poor" in Greek. The first is *penes*, which describes a person who works for a living and is by no means wealthy, but has what is needed. It is the second word for "poor" that Jesus uses in the text. *Ptoches*, which in the Greek literally means "to be destitute, powerless, and in need," goes far beyond simple humility. The distinction between the two meanings insists that a person can possess what he or she needs and still be considered "poor," but "destitute" is another matter.

Ptoches describes poverty as a condition with no recourse or help. People described by this term are completely at the mercy of others. This form of poverty drains life and leaves people utterly dependent. For Jesus to use such a word is striking both in its imagery and in its focus.[2]

Much like audiences in our own culture, Jesus' audience—especially those pious ones born of religion or great wealth—would have grown uncomfortable with such characterizations. For the Jew, poverty resulted in two effects. First, someone who is destitute lacks connection to the power structures, religious or civil. Second, without influence, one's poverty leads to oppression and the inability to rise above circumstances, literally leaving God as one's only advocate.

Please understand, Jesus does not condone or advocate physical poverty. Nowhere does Jesus support social structures that promote destitution or injustice. Quite the contrary, much of Jesus' ministry focuses on the state of the poor as a primary concern of the faithful. The elimination of physical poverty and injustice is one of the most prolific themes in Scripture, including the Gospels.[3]

As described in Barclay's Commentary, Jesus echoes the psalmist who described the poor as special to the heart of God. God *hears* the poor (Psalm 34:6) and *provides* for their needs (Psalm 68:10). God *defends* their lives (Psalm 72:4) and *satisfies* their hunger (Psalm 132:15). For the psalmist, a personal connection exists between God and the poor—loving, faithful, and intimate. In their *poverty*, the poor find their God (Psalm 105).

In this light, Jesus focuses on the power of spiritual poverty. Jesus illustrates this point in Mark 1:40-45 as he encounters a man with leprosy. As Jesus was entering the city, the man knelt before him and said, "If you choose, you can make me clean" (Mark 1:40). Now, the Bible is full of stories of Jesus' miracles and healings. In some cases, it is the faith of the person being healed that makes the difference. In others, it is the power and presence of God used as a teaching moment. And yet, in many, it is the pure compassion of Jesus for the people. However, this is the only account where the person in need challenges the actual *willingness* of Jesus to perform a miracle.

Perhaps it is odd to us who read the passage and know the many accounts of Jesus' healings, but for someone with leprosy, it was not an inappropriate question. In Jesus' day, having leprosy meant a life of pain, suffering and, in most instances, complete dependence on others. The man's residence at the city gate was not out of choice as much as out of placement. Anyone with leprosy was considered unclean and was relegated to the outskirts of towns and cities. And it wasn't just for sanitation issues. The religious leaders considered an unclean person to be an abomination to God. Thus, leprosy wasn't just an illness; it was a spiritual condition. Odds were, this man sat by the city gate for many years. I can imagine that he watched as countless individuals passed by, some with offerings of assistance, others with besieged looks, while still others gave no look at all. Sitting by the gate was a way of life—vulnerable, fragile, marginalized. Certainly, there had been other teachers too. The traffic of religious elite continued at a regular pace. Therefore, to inquire of Jesus' willingness was not an unusual question.

Yet accompanying the man's great needs is also a tremendous sense of faith. The second half of the statement says, "You can make me clean" (Mark 1:40). For the man with leprosy, his faith in Jesus' ability to heal was not the issue; it was his utter dependence on Jesus' willingness to do so. Of course, this begs the question of how much of the human soul the man could see that others could not. The man narrowed the issue down, not to ability, but to choice. He was completely at the mercy of Jesus' decision. This is the perfect example of the poverty of destitution—no alternative, no further options—the man's need far outweighed any form of self-reliance. This man absolutely needed Jesus. Beautifully, poetically, the rest of the scene unfolds: "Moved with pity, Jesus stretched out his hand and touched him, and said to him, 'I do choose. Be made clean!'" (Mark 1:41). The man's leprosy disappeared, and he was healed.

But even more significant, the man's poverty provided him freedom. With no pride, supposition, or personal ambition to get in the way, this man challenged Jesus and found him faithful.

Jesus transcends the theme of healthy, dependent spiritual poverty into a simple, more valuable principle—you will not find your life in things, materials, or even yourself, and this rings throughout Jesus' ministry, culminating in the pre-Crucifixion proclamation that those who want to truly find life must be willing to lose it. And so, in Jesus' use of "poor," he describes a person whose spirit is emptied to the point that only God remains. In essence, Jesus says one must be completely dependent on God in order to see the kingdom of heaven.[4]

Jesus issues the first blessing as a tension between the desire for personal fulfillment and the need for faithful and committed communion with God. In Matthew 5, the setting itself is emblematic of this poverty. The sermon is not in the grandeur of the Temple, but on a simple mountainside. Jesus' followers heard words born of personal language that spoke to the spiritual condition of all humanity. They heard not only the issues Jesus mentioned, but also the tone and character with which he addressed them. We cannot miss the personal needs of those who gathered. The listeners yearned for hope, equity, and a sense of purpose.

What sweet, but perplexing words they must have been for those whose lives drifted so far from meaning. These practical, pointed teachings remind us of the great worth we all hold in the eyes of God, whose purpose is that we experience the Kingdom. For three chapters, Matthew delineates, through the Sermon on the Mount, various topics—anger, adultery, divorce, vows, enemies, love, giving, prayer, fasting, money, relationship, faithfulness, and commitment—prevalent but complex issues. In the Beatitudes, as the opening words to the collection of teachings in the Sermon on the Mount, Jesus establishes the real nature of finding God and living in the Kingdom. The Blessings instill a spiritual code that allows us to see deeper through the spectacle of these forthcoming topics, not just merely as events or moral dilemmas, but as common conditions and possibilities for all human beings. And, more over, the first blessing is the formula by which a person begins the journey and, if properly applied and lived faithfully, transforms the ensuing topics into Kingdom discoveries.

The Mortgaged Life

A wonderful person with an exceptional gift for music, Mark had what appeared to be the perfect life. The father of five, he lived an exciting life as one of his company's top salesmen. In fact, Mark was considered one of the best in the country, and his demeanor showed it. He was not overly flashy, but Mark and his family lived a life full of *things*—cars, boats, houses. Like many of their age, Mark and his wife were not particularly irresponsible with money, but they made enough poor choices in their spending patterns to be what Mark himself described as *one breath away from destruction.* But in the highflying 1990s with stocks and incomes soaring, talk of such things seemed out of place and certainly unnecessary. Besides, Mark concealed rough edges of his life, while his daily routine suggested nothing other than smooth sailing and easy streets.

That is why many were stunned when they learned that Mark had secured more debt than he could manage, and that much of the debt was the result of a serious addiction to gambling. Gambling was not a significant issue in South Mississippi until the early 1990s when the quiet Mississippi Gulf Coast was transformed into one of the most prolific gambling areas in the country. One casino after another opened across the tranquil beaches of places named Biloxi, Gulfport, and Bay St. Louis. Once known more for shrimping and catastrophic hurricanes, the Gulf Coast changed, almost overnight, into a mini–Las Vegas minus the desert sands. The only industry that developed faster than casinos was pawn shops. Even now as I write these words, the coast deals with the wake of a massive hurricane. But even with the casinos in ruins, the gaming industry plans an even more extensive influence in the future.

Returning from seminary two years after the first casino opened, I was shocked at the number of families and individuals touched by gambling addictions. And these families were not strangers. People I had known my whole life lost everything to this invisible malady. Mark was another one of its victims, and he was waiting at my office early on a Thursday morning. Standing in front of me was not the self-confident, vibrant person we all knew, but a wounded soul, repressed by the weight of the world. Clearly shocked by his appearance, I quickly ushered him inside. He looked as though he had not slept in days. The night before, Mark's wife had taken the children and left for her parents' home in Jackson. Two days prior, Mark admitted his problem with gambling, and the myriad of dominoes began to fall. They were mortgaged to the hilt and had credit card debt in the amount of $100,000. The interest alone on the various cards and lines of credit consumed over half of their income. To make matters worse, Mark borrowed money from a disreputable businessperson after a particularly bad night at the roulette tables. But nothing could prepare me for his next confession. Seemingly, several weeks earlier, while celebrating a *winning night*, Mark, in a drunken stupor, had a relationship with a young woman he met at the casino. Mark had learned earlier in the week that she was pregnant.

We talked for several hours about options for his family, the young lady in question, and Mark's financial future. I was a young associate pastor just out of seminary, and my wife (a schoolteacher at the time) and I were barely getting by, but I wanted to help. I asked Mark if there was anything we could do. I even told him that I had a few hundred dollars saved and would be glad to loan the money to him. Mark looked at me, trying to remain gracious, and said, "Thanks, but I am afraid your offer is just pennies, my friend."

As I sat listening to Mark, I noticed that he constantly wrung his hands. He was nervous, out of sorts, and lost. The façade of his life betrayed him, and now, he was unable to find the core, that life jacket to embrace for safety. Strangely enough, as I continued to watch his hands, Mark appeared more like a child than an adult whose world was crumbling. In the rush to what he believed was a significant life, Mark surrendered his values for lies. And I realized that worse than his leveraged financial picture, Mark somewhere along the way leveraged his life.

Within the next year, Mark and his wife divorced, and he was forced to take bankruptcy. Unable to work, Mark retreated into alcohol as a means of medicating himself against the ache of past mistakes. In the ensuing months, he began several tours through various rehabs and twelve step programs. For several years, Mark's journey took him to places that only Dante could visualize. The road was difficult and, at times, almost hopeless. Eventually, I lost touch with Mark, but I continued to wonder where his journey might lead.

Years and many prayers later, Mark called unexpectedly. He was living in a small town in the panhandle of Florida. While visiting through Hattiesburg, he invited me to have a cup of coffee. I was excited to hear from him, but somewhat anxious about what I would find.

Much to my amazement, Mark appeared not only healthy, but also *healed.* He said that several years ago, after migrating to Florida, searching for work and also running from back child support and debt collectors, he considered his life at a critical crossroads. A coincidental meeting of a fellow but recovering addict at a Tallahassee McDonald's led Mark to a Christian rehab center. To his surprise, the Christian rehab "boot camp," as he called it, saved his life. Placing a high premium on addressing the cause and not just the symptoms of Mark's life, they focused less on the sickness and more on the cure. One year later, Mark emerged a changed person, his life pieced together. He married a wonderful Christian woman. Although it is difficult and his former wife remains extremely bitter, Mark stays in close contact with his children. He is working again but, this time, as a marketing director for a nonprofit organization devoted to helping people put their lives back together. And, most important, Mark is sober and hasn't gambled in years.

However, the most impressive part of Mark's story was not so much the details of his life but his spirit. No longer did he talk about life as a game or competition. Possessions no longer defined him, and he was no longer enamored with the latest trend or get rich quick scheme. He cared little about how the neighbors lived, except to meet them at the local support group, and he spoke carefully and meaningfully about life, family, and love. No, Mark spoke differently because he valued different things, and to be quite honest, it looked good on him. As we left the coffee shop that morning, Mark gave me a big hug, invited our family to visit if we were ever in Florida, and thanked me for my prayers. Then as we began to walk our separate ways, he turned and said, "Preacher Man [a name he always called me], tell folks that sometimes you have to lose everything to find the most precious gift God gives us . . . Him!"

Hope for Riches Unseen

The Sermon on the Mount echoes the dilemma between a complex world and simple, beautiful treasures resting around us. However, in this first blessing, Jesus reminded us that God blesses those who understand the simple, dependent nature of life. He connected moral teaching with grace by reminding the listeners that real life finds expression first in relationship and obedience to God. The listener attains the far-reaching principles mentioned throughout the Sermon on the Mount by sub-scribing first to what it means to be a part of God's family. These rela-tionships include difficult, hot topics such as divorce, tithing, and deceit. Yet they exemplify how life's values become unraveled and tattered when we disconnect from our source of purpose and meaning. Sound familiar?

For many in Jesus' generation, the principles of the law overshadowed the imprint of grace that gives a glimpse of God. For these persons, God represented a *rule* and was experienced more as a *distant figure* than the personal and present Creator. When people reduce relationship with God to a series of *legal obligations*, they miss the intent of the law, which is to preserve the deep connections to God and neighbor. Ultimately, the Sermon on the Mount is about life principles, not rules. The purpose of the teachings is to reconnect us to the heart and life of God. They remind us not only of the *how* of living, but also of the *purpose* of living For years, I studied the Sermon on the Mount by separating the Beatitudes (or Blessings) from the life lessons that follow. However, doing this is a mistake. The Beatitudes are treasures. In them, Jesus teaches us that we cannot live life unless we are able to first get our hearts and souls around certain basic, soul-connecting truths that generate deep but enlightening questions. What becomes of great success if we have forgotten how to cherish simplicity? What becomes of those with great wealth if they have forgotten the nature of real poverty? What becomes of true relationship in this world if one forgets the real essence of humil-ity and sacrifice? What becomes of the spiritual disciplines if one refuses to live a righteous and pure life? What becomes of our relationship with God if we miss, first, the intimate connection between God and our neighbor? Jesus teaches us about the world's spiritual riches by helping us first to see the value in life's simple, most elementary expressions.

The first blessing of Jesus highlights this understanding. *Blessed are those who realize their need for God.* It is simple, profound, and the begin-ning of true transformation. But the race for possessions dominates our culture, and we continually discover the finish line empty and meaning-less.[5] Why can the Jennifers, the Marks, and even the people with leprosy of this world see the value of life so much easier than we? Because their worlds are not leveraged by selfishness and expectation. They see each day's possibilities wrapped tenderly in the utter dependency of human existence. But for many of us, as one life choice lands upon another, our obligations to shame, disappointment, and self-sufficiency drown our ability to see the promise in each new day. We become spiritual debtors to unseen, innumerable spiritual creditors. Eventually, we masquerade as mature, healthy adults, all the while mortgaging our souls the same as many of us mortgage our bank accounts.

Thus, Jesus begins his teaching ministry with the hope that what we cannot locate in the world, we can find in God—no, let me say it more directly—we can find only in God! However, we must be willing to place our whole trust in God's provisions. By supplanting our worldly possessions, we find that which is more fulfilling; by becoming helpless, we discover our greatest source of strength; and by obeying God, we become free. And so, Jesus proclaims, in having nothing, we discover everything.

Notes

1. Annie Dillard, *Pilgrim at Tinker Creek* (New York: HarperPerennial, 1998), 17.
2. William Barclay, *The Gospel of Matthew*, vol. 1 (Louisville: Westminster John Knox Press, 2001), 104-5.
3. *Interpreter's Commentary*, 280.
4. Barclay, *Gospel of Matthew*, 107.
5. *Interpreter's Commentary*, 280.

The Second Blessing
Joy Learned Only from Sorrow

Blessed are those who mourn, for they will be comforted.
—Matthew 5:4

Within your secrets, lies your sickness.
—Abraham Verghese[1]

Mourning scares us. It is a unique human emotion, sitting somewhere between the bliss of love and the stark drama of fear. Mourning is that motionless moment of the human heart whereby we can both sense and experience our surroundings, but cannot seem to penetrate their meaning. As one friend put it, it is an open door to a deeper part of us that is incredibly fragile and wary, but it is also strangely inviting. Many times, this door serves as our guide for discovering lessons about ourselves, others, and the world that we never could have learned otherwise.

I never really experienced grief's power until the death of a dear friend several years ago. Her loss was so sudden and tragic that the world seemed to slow and there was a watching quality to life. The watching quality is the feeling of standing outside oneself, viewing the events and circumstances as though one were an unseen observer. In the stillness of the moment, mourning also unveiled profound lessons in life—most particularly the depth of love experienced only through great loss.

However, throughout my ministry, I never understood this lesson or why Jesus, in this second beatitude, connected mourning with such joy. To say the least, the second beatitude remained a mystery. It seemed unrealistic in a world filled with so much sorrow. I held too many hands and shared too many last embraces before death took its toll, on those who departed in those final moments and on the ones left behind, to think of mourning as blessed. In my opinion, mourning left only brokenness and despair and had no redeeming quality. I struggled with this throughout each episode of loss or suffering I experienced, including my grandmother's final days. For me, mourning held no quality other than a deep imperfection threaded through the fabric of life.

Tom

The phone rang much earlier than usual, and I was surprised at the voice on the other end. It was raspy and the breathing labored. If not for the rich and distinct Southern drawl, I might not have known who was calling.

"Shane, I am sorry to call so early. However, I know that you are very busy and I wanted to catch you before you left for the day. Would it be possible for us to sit a while?"

"To sit a while" was rural Southern for "to have a conversation." "To have a talk" did not convey the importance of what needed to be said, and "conversation" seemed too formal. "To sit a while" spoke to the setting and to the nature of the topic. The caller had something on his mind, and he needed to talk about it fairly soon. Reaching for my Coke bottle glasses to notice the time, I replied, "Sure, Tom, when would you like to meet?"

Prior to my grandmother's death, I had not heard from Tom in several years. Seeing him at the funeral surprised and pleased me. He played a significant role in my earlier life. A lively character with a gregarious smile and infectious laugh, Tom knew how to keep the party going well into the night. People came from miles around just to listen to one of his fantastic stories. Although their accuracy remains in question, they seemed gospel truth to a young boy of seven.

Tom was a big man, whose oversized hands reminded me of the hands of a cartoon character with their thick fingers and overly callused palms. Weathered by years of hard work and faithful discipline to his craft, these hands were hard not to notice and even harder to forget. Over the years, the wrinkle and thickness of his hands traced to his face and brow. Tom's large jaws seemed more like jowls. Add to this a pug nose and deep brown eyes, and Tom's face reminded me of a bulldog. But his spirit said something else. Tom loved life and laughed often. He loved people and people loved him.

Aged, worn, and nearly eighty-five years old, Tom moved slower now. Seeing him at my grandmother's funeral emphasized the passage of time, but when he laughed, it transported me back to my childhood, and amidst the coffin, flowers, and surreal nature of death, I felt the mood and situation lighten. His presence provided a needed respite from the usual drudgery that so often enfolds such moments. But it was a brief encounter, and following those final words and handshakes, each of us returned to his normal routine.

Therefore, one can imagine my surprise, several weeks later, at Tom's invitation to meet and talk. Around lunch I arrived at his small, box-shaped home, which stood just off a dirt road in a rural south Mississippi county. I had never been to his home before, but Tom's directions were impeccable. As I made my way to the modest white house, Tom met me at the door, waved at me with his cane, and bellowed a hearty "hello." He invited me into his kitchen, and we sat at what appeared to be a 1960s breakfast table, surrounded by aluminum chairs covered in a green plastic material. The décor suggested that little had changed for Tom over the past forty years.

"Your grandmother sent me one of these about a year ago," Tom said, holding up one of the self-published devotional books I coauthored several years earlier. "Good stuff. Especially enjoyed the story about the redhead and the mule." Tom chuckled while I remembered my devotion about a young girl that I admired whose beauty was not matched by her singing. One day during church, she provided special music only to find herself in competition with a braying mule just outside the window. The whole experience was quite funny.

"Your grandmother was very special, but I guess you know that," Tom said. "She meant a great deal to a lot of us. She was especially proud of you." I had heard this phrase what seemed hundreds of times over those days during my grandmother's funeral.

"Yes, sir," I said, trying to appear humble and also trying to hold back the emotion that seemed to rush forward every time someone told me.

"But I didn't ask you here just to tell you that," Tom stated. "No, I wanted to tell you about your grandmother and about what a difference she made in our lives—all of us who knew her." Tom paused and then, after clearing his throat, continued, "She understood people...right here [pointing at his heart]. She knew how to get into their souls. That is a real gift...most people can't or at least won't try to do that anymore."

I had heard the various stories about my grandmother's encouragement, prayers, and concern for others, but Tom wasn't just speaking for the collective group—he was talking about himself.

"She knew me... too well. You see, I was a hell raiser when I was your age. Thought I had the world by the tail, but it had me."

My mind drifted, trying to catch a glimpse of this man, who had appeared old my entire life, as some sort of rabble-rouser. Tom, seeing the distance in my eyes, touched my arm and spoke, "I was on a rough path there for a while, and everybody had given up on me... everyone but your grandmother."

Tom told me how he had known my family since his childhood. Living in a small community provided the advantage of tending to everyone's business on a regular basis. No chamber of commerce was needed in rural, southern Mississippi!

"I knew your grandfather. Meanest SOB anyone could ever be around. Most of us knew about his blood condition and always thought the morphine kept him so angry, but still, we felt bad for your grandmother. People didn't just leave a marriage in those days." Tom sat a moment and took another breath.

I never knew my maternal grandfather. He died when my mother was a child; however, the stories of his brutality and philandering were legend in the family. Officials called his death a suicide, but local gossip assumed he had been killed by a jealous husband or angry brother. Not many mourned his passing.

Following his sudden death, my grandmother resumed her education, which had been placed on hold by her uncooperative husband. Stories abound of her riding in the back of a laundry truck to and from college to earn her degree as a teacher. Following graduation, she taught for nearly forty years, shaping the lives of generations of young children throughout the area.

Several years after being widowed, she found a man whom many considered to be the love of her life, Creighton. A large teddy bear of a figure, he was a member of a neighboring county's sheriff department. His demeanor suited my grandmother perfectly, and more than one person talked of never seeing her happier than when she was with him. Unfortunately, not many years after they married, Creighton died suddenly of a heart attack. Until the day she died, my grandmother talked about him with fondness and an unmistakable, true love. For such a faithful woman, her life was filled with an incredible amount of loss.

Tom's conversation resumed and shook me from my private thoughts. "One night I was in a stupor at one of the local juke joints, when in walks Dorothy and Creighton. I was moving and slobbering on one of the stools at the end of the bar when I saw her coming. She grabbed me by the hair on the back of my head and proceeded to drag me out of that place. Most humiliating thing that's ever happened to me . . . and it probably saved my life." Tom stopped. I could tell that he needed to catch his breath. But I was caught by the image of my gentle grandmother dragging someone out of a bar.

"My grandmother did this? Dragged you out?" I said, disbelieving.

Tom smiled and said, "Yep; she always told me that if she heard of me in one of those shacks again, I had better pray that Creighton got to me first. Unfortunately, that night, Creighton was about five steps behind her." We both laughed. "Your grandmother didn't just talk the talk. She walked it and whooped it when need be. She was a wonderful, sweet lady, but she could also be tough when it came to something she believed in."

I needed to let this sink in. I had known my grandmother from one point of view, that of a child and then as a young adult, with her getting older and more deliberate. To think that she was such a *fireball* was hard to imagine but not to believe. I knew my grandmother lived her values faithfully. She believed in them as more than just beliefs. Her values were a source of strength and guidance. She knew what she believed to be right and what she knew to be wrong.

"Your grandmother taught me that life is about staying true to your values and being able to believe in something bigger than yourself," Tom said seriously. "She didn't have an easy life. In fact, it was very hard. But she never gave away her values or her hope, and she served as an example to the rest of us to not give up either. Boy, I'm here today because your grandmother was willing to grab me by the hair of my head and drag me to a better life, even if I was kicking and screaming."

Tom and I talked for nearly an hour about my grandmother, her friendship, and his subsequent years of sobriety and faithfulness. When I got ready to leave, he walked me to the door and said, "Thanks for coming to talk to an old man. I just wanted you to know that your grandmother was no ordinary lady."

I nodded in agreement and moved toward the door. Just then, Tom said something else, something my soul had needed to hear for several weeks since I stood at her coffin with that horrible, empty feeling in my gut. "She was a real precious jewel in this world, refined by a lot of fire, but always coming out stronger and more beautiful. I just thank God that she was willing to endure it and willing to rejoice while it was happening so that the rest of us could see by its reflection."

And with that, my question was answered—why my grandmother could speak of God's grace as a precious gift even while she was dying. Why she could speak of forgiveness for her abusive first husband. Why she could smile and thank God for the years she had with Creighton instead of protesting bitterly against time cut short. Why she could look life in the face and not be hindered by its limitations or troubles. Why she could see the best in everyone, even those who many of us didn't believe deserved it. It was because when she saw the world, she saw it the way Jesus did, and she knew that each day was an opportunity for us to see it too.

Comfort from Sorrow

Matthew translates Jesus' Aramaic word for "mourning" into the strongest Greek equivalent possible.[2] The image is of one who endures the loss of that which is most dear. It is an almost paralyzing, life-numbing form of grief. Death drags from each of us profound memories and stings us with loss. But when one delves further, death is not the only cause for the mourning Jesus speaks about in the second beatitude. Such mourning also emerges from the general suffering of the world—from the plight of persons who are victims of injustice and despair and from our personal sense of loss that comes as a result of bad life decisions and mistakes. Jesus broadens the picture of mourning from the vivid scenes of a tomb to the consequences of life's poorest choices or circumstances. It is a personal view of grief from which no one is immune, for Jesus knows we have all lost someone or something that causes our lives to be less than whole.

But with such an expression of mourning comes an equally powerful view of God's comfort. Jesus approaches the vulnerability of life honestly and gives us a glimpse of why loving and living, even with the prospect of such pain, offer real comfort. And this is not a *cheap* comfort, feelings spoken as mere clichés, but a sincere embrace of unconditional love, the source of life's deepest emotions.[3]

Jesus encourages us to love with real openness and honesty, but such love also brings great vulnerability. I know what you are asking: "What happens when one loves to the point of such great risk? Does one avoid the pain and struggle of this world?" Quite the contrary. Jesus tells his disciples that in this world they will have trouble, but there is also potential for great joy as Jesus assures them to take heart because he has overcome the world (see John 16:33). Sure, the risk of grief or mourning can be overwhelming, but God promises life-changing joy if we are willing to take the chance.

The life that risks love to the point of real vulnerability shifts the world's expectations about love. By risking our own grief, we see the possibility of genuine relationship and community, of sincere faith and spiritual connection—as God intended from the beginning. We should not miss the declarative tone of Jesus' second blessing—*Blessed are those who mourn, for they* will be *comforted*. Certainly, Jesus affirms the presence of mourning in this world, and the risk of love that often leads to such emotions, but equally affirming is the promise of spectacular comfort born from the heart of God. God calls us to risk ourselves not for the mere *possibility* of comfort, but in the certainty of it.

We see this time and again as Jesus confronts the mourning of this world, whether in the death of a friend (Lazarus) or in the grief of a people's discontent (weeping over Jerusalem). It is even present in Jesus' discourse about his own suffering and death. In Matthew 9:15 and John 16:16-22, he teaches his disciples about suffering from a very personal perspective, referring to a time when he will no longer be with them. Jesus promises, however, that their mourning will turn to comfort—an unimaginable joy that the world will not understand (John 16).

Often we cannot or will not experience this kind of comfort and joy because we have opted for a safer or easier path complete with little risk or a quick fix. These options unfortunately set up a false sense of security. Some may think they can prevent the risk of grief by refusing to love completely, but ultimately, this takes the form of a more profound grief— loneliness and unfulfillment. No, the joy of which I speak is born only from the risk of possibly losing it. However, the life, death, and resurrection of Jesus bridge the distance between mourning and comfort, between sorrow and joy. Jesus calls us to see the path and to courageously walk down it.

A Single Tree

Down a hidden, two-lane highway, between two small towns in North Mississippi, rests some of the most beautiful landscape you will ever see. Large, open fields, quaint farmhouses, and sturdy hardwoods with fall colors that rival any found along the Natchez Trace dominate the scenery. Several Novembers ago, while driving this route, a young pastor noticed one of these fields set against the backdrop of a modest white farmhouse. The home itself sat perched on a hill toward the back of the property with a variety of trees and shrubs decorating its perimeter, creating a sort of foliage oasis. The field in front ran for several hundred feet from the road to the front steps, and was populated only by a single oak tree sitting perfectly in the middle.

Throughout the Mississippi Delta, it is not uncommon to see an open field interspersed with a few trees, the leftover of forests long cleared to make room for planting. It is also not uncommon to find single trees in large expanses of fields left generations before as shade for workers seeking relief from the sun. However, in a day of technology and amazing equipment, with most farms requiring more machine than man power, these lonesome trees appear weathered and wearied from single-handedly catching the brunt of too many storms.

Yet the tree in this particular open expanse was unique. First, it was not old as oaks go, maybe twenty-five or thirty years since it was planted. Second, it didn't sit in a planting field like the ones to the left and right of the farmhouse. So the tree was most probably not used as shade for workers. The tree sat almost at the geographic center of the parcel of what appeared to be no more than a large front yard. And finally, hanging from the young branches was a rope swing, partnered nearby with a child's play set. All of this seemed out of place and somewhat confusing. Although the young man slowed down enough to catch the basic details, he did not stop. But that did not prevent the questions.

Continuing to his meeting, the young pastor wondered about this lonesome tree, so perfect but so awkward in this large field. Clearly, it had been placed there, but by whom and for what purpose? For several miles and through the entire meeting, he thought about every possible scenario, trying to imagine the story behind this tree. Yes, it occurred to him that he might be making too much of this, that he had too much time on his hands, and that the answer was probably simple. But the tree intrigued him and so he decided to stop at the farmhouse on the return trip and ask about it.

The young pastor rarely did anything like this, and he especially never recommended that anyone stop at a stranger's door in rural Mississippi. Although most people are incredibly hospitable and known for kindness to strangers, such an inquiry would appear bereft of good judgment. Sensing this reasonably in his head, though, did not alter his curiosity or overcome his reason. Given this, the young "theologian turned detective" pulled down the long driveway, drove past the lonesome tree, and proceeded to the front door.

Stepping up on the front porch, he heard and felt the creaking of the wood beneath his feet. It was a porch that had been well taken care of for many years, but now it was in some need of repair. The young pastor knocked two or three times, before a small older woman opened the front door. The silver-haired lady looked to be in her late seventies or early eighties, frail and slow, but not feeble by any means. She had a delicate beauty unmasked by makeup or jewelry.

"May I help you?" she said softly, still safely behind a locked screen door.

"Good afternoon, ma'am," he said, somewhat nervous at this seemingly absurd scene. "I was passing by your place on my way to a meeting, and I noticed how beautiful your home is." The woman seemed puzzled by the simplicity of the answer. The young man continued, "And I was especially curious because of the one oak tree that seems so . . . unique sitting in the middle of your yard." He knew this was not the best intro, and he was afraid that he had only confused the situation more. "I know the thought of a stranger stopping to talk about a tree seems . . . well, odd." The young pastor paused at the thought.

After a few moments, the woman unveiled a subtle smile and, without saying a word, unlocked the screen door and stepped outside. The young man backed up as she motioned for him to move to his right and take a seat. They sat on two wooden rockers sitting side by side with only a small iron-legged table in between. Her rocker, the one to the left, seemed to fit her fragile frame. It was worn, but to her proportions, and he could tell that she enjoyed the feel of its familiarity. His rocker seemed uncomfortable to him, obviously built for someone else. They rocked for a few moments, while the lady looked at the lonesome tree in her front yard.

"I haven't had anyone ask about that tree in while," the woman said softly. "At least not since my husband passed away last year. We would sit here during those last days while he was so sick and all. He loved to rock and hold hands and stare out at the landscape. You have a pretty keen eye," the woman said, shifting the topic. "What did you say you did for a living?"

The young pastor had not told her, but decided to use the minister card in case she thought he was some lunatic. "I am a Methodist minister," he said. "I don't preach in a local church right now, but I travel to different churches teaching about spiritual formation."

She looked at her new young friend the same way his great-aunt did when he, having grown up a Baptist, first told her that he was becoming a Methodist. A staunch Baptist, his aunt just stared at him with equal parts confusion and pity, without once differentiating which she felt more.

"So you are a minister but you don't preach in a church?" the woman said spryly.

"Yes, ma'am," he said, waiting for the response.

"Um!" was her reply. *What did that mean*, he thought.

Trying to push the subject in a new direction, the young pastor uttered, "You said that no one has asked about the tree. I take it there is a story behind it?" He offered this request half wanting to know the story and half wanting to validate his own sense about it, realizing that his greatest fear would have been to discover that the tree was, in fact, storyless.

"Oh, yes, there is a story," the woman said. "The tree was planted in memory of our only child, Todd. He was killed thirty-five years ago while on his way from Memphis. Police say a drunk driver hit him somewhere around Tunica. He was a student at Ole Miss, and they were playing football up there. That was back in the days of Archie Manning. Hard to believe that he has two boys in the NFL." The woman stopped and looked at the young man, who was more than a little shocked by the statement, but only for a moment. Two things reigned supreme in North Mississippi—cotton and Ole Miss football. The young pastor agreed with her surprise and she continued.

"We were devastated, especially my husband. He would just wander around out in the fields for hours. I never saw him cry, but I know he did. He was a very proud man. He and Todd had a good relationship, but it had never been all it could be. My husband worked very hard, and there was always something to be done on a farm. It left little time for playing or having fun. Farming is just a tough life." She paused, and the young pastor realized that she, too, was deeply engaged in the image of her own story.

"Our nephew's wife gave us an oak tree to plant in Todd's memory. At first, we thought about planting it at the entrance of the cemetery where we buried him. However, one morning I came out and Earl, my husband, was busy planting it in the middle of the front field. I watched as he meticulously stepped off the perimeter until he had found the exact center. As he finished planting, he walked to the barn, replaced all of the planting equipment, and then came in for breakfast. We didn't say a word the entire day."

The young pastor sat there trying to fix the scene of this grieving father planting the tree that would remind him of his only child. Sitting on the porch, the pastor realized because of where the father planted it, there was precisely no angle from which it could not be seen.

"It was days before he even mentioned it," the woman said. "Then one morning while we were sitting right here," she motioned to the rockers, "he told me why he planted it there." At this moment, the young pastor, too, found himself sitting forward in the chair.

"He told me how all those years when Todd was a young boy, he would ask his father to come out and play—football, baseball, whatever the season. However, with so much to be done around the farm, chores took precedence over fun, and so my husband, who felt his own chores never ended, always found something else to occupy his time. Earl would talk about walking around the corner of the house and seeing Todd toss up a baseball, only to have to catch it himself, or punt a football, forced to retrieve it from where it landed." The woman stopped and looked intently at the open field, raising the index finger of her right hand from the chair's handle. "That field represented a lifetime of missed opportunities to my husband, Reverend. I know he planted that tree in the center of that field partly as a memorial, but also partly as a form of punishment."

The young pastor sat back in the chair and tried to take in what he had just heard. He had imagined what could be the purpose behind the tree, but nothing had prepared him for the truth. Sometimes our wildest fiction cannot emulate the real world for its opulent and often painful facts. And now it hit him—every time her husband sat on this porch, now years past prime for planting and farming, her husband would have to look at that tree and remember. The father may have missed his son's life, but he would never allow himself to be free of his son's death.

The lady and he sat for a few moments in the quiet. A gentle breeze had begun to blow, and there was an eerie peace on that porch in North Mississippi. "May I ask one other question?" the young pastor said in a quiet voice. "What about the play set?" The lady developed the strangest expression, part revelation and part fulfillment as though she knew he would ask the question.

"In 1994, my husband and I were sitting on the porch one morning having our coffee, when a car pulled down the road. Out stepped a familiar, handsome young man accompanied by a young woman and a small child. They were clean-cut and appeared well-to-do. As I told you earlier, we don't get much company, so it was unusual to have visitors. We invited them to the porch. Personally, I thought they were lost until . . ." The woman again paused, and he could tell that every time she talked about this moment it was an opportunity to visualize and relive.

"Until?" he asked.

"Until the young man called us by our names, and as he walked closer, I thought I was seeing a ghost. The young man was the spitting image of Todd." For the first time, the woman looked the young pastor directly in the eyes and said, "It was Todd's son." For a minute, the young pastor thought he was caught in some soap opera episode, but he could tell that the woman was very serious.

"His son?" he murmured.

The woman continued, "We knew that Todd had been seeing someone in Memphis. In fact, that was the real reason he had gone the night he was killed. The young woman was from a very wealthy family and had gotten pregnant. Todd and she were working through the details of what to do next, including planning to elope the week after he died. When Todd was killed, the girl's parents convinced her not to tell us about the baby, and they agreed to raise the child. At first, I couldn't imagine anyone doing such a thing to people, but after thinking about it, I can understand their fear and confusion. The girl had the baby, a boy, and eventually married and moved to Mobile, Alabama. She named the baby Eric Todd."

The young pastor sat amazed at the story, wishing to soak up the entire episode, transfixed by the seemingly implausible, yet beautiful details.

The woman finished: "Eventually, the young man, who goes by Eric, discovered the truth about his father and decided to find us. He was married by then and had a small son named Jack. Over the years, Eric has been very faithful about coming to see us, and his family spends a great deal of time here at the farm. Jack loved the place and..." The woman's voice broke. "Especially his great-grandfather. They would play for hours in the open field, chasing dogs, running after fly balls and, yes...," she looked over at the young man, "sitting under that tree playing on the play set that my husband built."

The woman and the young pastor sat for another hour talking about life and its interesting twists and turns. He told her about his family, and she politely endured as he showed her pictures of his daughters. She informed him that Eric had three children now, three sons to be exact, and that he and his family lived in a suburb of Memphis. However, she was very proud of the fact that Eric visited regularly and was now the manager of her estate and the farm's affairs. "He wants me to come live with him," she said smilingly, "but I could never leave this place." The young pastor noticed she uttered these words while looking directly at that single tree.

What Shall We Say About Such Things?

I have often begun eulogies with these words from the apostle Paul: "What then are we to say about these things?" (Romans 8:31). It is a question he asks about the nature of life and the distinct possibility that

Christians will face great hardships during their journey. I have yet to preside at a funeral that these words did not seem fitting or poignant. Death, grief, and loss stun us, knock us off our feet. To be strong and not feel the pain is a form of spiritual lying, and so, those who seem to grieve best are those who grieve honestly. That is exactly Paul's lament—we cannot face life unless we are willing to face all of it, imperfections included.

Jesus offers another part of the story, a blessing so profound and important for the human experience that in its rule is one of the most valuable lessons we learn in order to experience the full nature of God's presence within us. We learn to live and love to the point of great vulnerability, even to the point of risking the pain of loss, so that we might experience the blessing of life at its fullest. No relationship, whether with God or another human being, can be whole unless we set aside our protective gates and give ourselves freely to the experience of it all.

Yes, the downside is the risk of hurt, loss, and pain, but Jesus answers the sting of death and mourning with the assurance of comfort, the likes of which the world cannot understand. God has not forgotten our brokenness, and God is aware of our pain.

I realize now that Jesus taught this value so that we would not sacrifice love and life in order to avoid pain and grief. God has chosen not to forsake us, but instead has given that burden to Jesus on Calvary. But through Christ's burden, all believers face the world with a hope that transcends a broken heart and transforms our lament. "What then are we to say about these things?" Paul continues in Romans 8:31, "If God is for us, who is against us?" Indeed!

Notes

1. Abraham Verghese, *The Tennis Partner* (New York: HarperCollins, 1998), 374.

2. William Barclay, *The Gospel of Matthew*, vol. 1 (Louisville: Westminster John Knox Press, 2001), 107.

3. *Interpreter's Commentary*, 282.

The Third Blessing
The Balanced Life

Blessed are the meek, for they will inherit the earth.
—Matthew 5:5

To live by grace means to acknowledge my whole life story,
the light side and the dark.
—Brennan Manning[1]

Three Days, Three Obituaries

Nothing does death better than the *New York Times* obituaries page. The memorials, although brief, are well written and share a glimpse into the lives of various individuals, famous, infamous, and everything in between. Within a span of three days in late May of 2005, the newspaper posted obituaries for three significant individuals—Eddie, Oscar, and Eliot.

Eddie Albert had been a star of television, stage, and film for nearly seventy years when he passed away at the age of ninety-nine. His most famous role, at least for my generation, was that of Oliver on the hit CBS sitcom *Green Acres* from 1965 to 1971. Who could forget his portrayal of a wealthy New York lawyer's experience of farm life? Eddie also played dozens of roles from stage to the big screen, including one of my favorites as the maniacal warden in 1974's *The Longest Yard.* His remarkable acting career will not soon be forgotten in its significant impact of bringing laughter to millions everywhere.[2]

Oscar Brown Jr. was a singer, playwright, songwriter, and actor known for his unique mix of music and the arts with social activism. When he died in Chicago at the age of seventy-eight, most described Oscar as a mix between jazz singer and storyteller. A versatile entertainer, Oscar loved performing for people and providing a sense of both escape and poignancy to those who enjoyed his work. He was known especially for bringing the issue of gang violence among young African American teens to the forefront. The *New York Times* listed Oscar as a major cultural force in Chicago.[3]

The final significant person was named Eliot. Although Eliot did not receive multiple columns in the *New York Times* upon his death, his significance is more than evident in the small obituary of less than one hundred words. Eliot died at the age of 101 and was the "beloved husband of Florence, father of Av, grandfather of Mark and adored uncle of many nieces and nephews and their children, and many friends." But as poignant as this statement was, listen to the rest of the obituary: "He was a life-loving, people-loving citizen of New York City. His warmth and wit and generosity towards the world and towards people in particular will be remembered always."[4] Could anyone ask for a better description or tribute? Probably not. Sure, there were no accolades or notable achievements according to the world's standards. Eliot was not a well-known actor, celebrated musician, or famous social activist, but one would be hard-pressed to consider his life anything other than significant.

Three days, three obituaries, three significant lives. How does one measure the success or failure of a human life? The question puzzles us, especially given the unique and daunting nature of the standards of the world. At the end of a life, is our existence on this planet gauged only by a résumé or vita? Those who loved Eliot would argue, "Certainly not!"

The Balanced Life

The word *meek* reminds me of the character Lennie from John Steinbeck's *Of Mice and Men*. In this book, Steinbeck depicts a hulking, yet gentle, developmentally delayed man. Lennie was large in stature, but his limited cognitive abilities showed an elementary, naïve approach to life and, unfortunately, an impression of insignificance.

Another example of *meek* was one of my former grade school teachers. She was small, frail, and very bright, but she looked almost mousy. Her voice was not loud enough nor her temperament bold enough to keep order in her classroom. After only a couple of years of teaching, she left the classroom to become a librarian. People said her *meek* nature fit well in her new environment, the library.

Meek, no matter how we phrase, describe, or define it, in our culture generally indicates some deficiency. We do not celebrate or embrace the virtues of meekness because we are convinced that a more confident approach to life must be better. To most of us, *meek* means to be stepped on and forgotten, living as second-class citizens in a first-class world.

Matthew 5:5 offers another way to understand the meek of this world. The Greek word *praus*, used to translate Jesus' Aramaic, provides a multidimensional view of those called "gentle and lowly." In fact, the description is not negative at all, but seen as a positive way of life. For those in Jesus' day, *praus* expressed a deeply ethical form of living that balanced the great extremes of overabundance and deficiency. But the meaning also spoke to the need for self-control and for the eradication of pride in order for one's life to be complete. People, who were described as *praus*, lived balanced lives, fully aware of their own weaknesses but confident in their circumstances because they knew their relationship to God and trusted the ways of God's kingdom.[5]

By contrast, the arrogant life exists wildly between having too much and never being satisfied. It relies on pride as the barometer for success and failure. Our world rewards these individuals for their assertiveness and drive, but in God's equation, balance trumps acquisition every time. The meek understand full well the fleeting values of most of the world's treasures. The world's treasures belong to the high and mighty, but the greatest treasure, relationship with God and life lived God's way, belongs to those whose perspective is endowed with grace instead of position. Those forgotten or pushed aside by the expectations of this world experience a cosmic shift in both stature and priority in the eyes of God through the redemption of Christ. And through this, God restores the fortunes not only of the meek, but also of the entire world.[6]

The prophetic nature of Christ's third blessing shifts the balance for those who are undervalued in this world. It is a clarion call for justice, peace, and reconciliation. The third blessing recalibrates the way we view significance for our personal lives and our communal lives. The world says "gather all you can" while Jesus counters with "gather enough for you and for others." The world wishes for us to sacrifice the means in order to validate the ends. Jesus pleads that the means ultimately are the ends. The world promises temporal fame and success. Jesus ensures that what we find deepest within us and within each other is what lasts forever.

Therefore, what does it mean to be meek in the eyes of Jesus? Those who have placed their lives upon God's redeeming grace, wherever their paths may lead, speak of a strength neither cultivated nor appreciated by the world. Elsewhere, Jesus said, "Those who find their life will lose it" (Matthew 10:39), "But many who are first will be last, and the last will be first" (Matthew 19:30), and "So the *last* will be first, and the first will be last" (Matthew 20:16, emphasis added). These expressions may mean little or seem crazy alongside the world's mantra of "win at all costs," but that is what makes Jesus' message so unique and so inviting. It is inclusive, open, and hopeful. It transforms our understanding of what is truly significant in this world: relationship with God and living life in God's ways of mercy, justice, and peace.

A Parade of Homemade Stars

Their float was not spectacular or particularly unique, but there was still something special about this group of schoolchildren, something that caught your attention as they moved down Main Street in the town's Christmas parade. The sign on the yellow school bus read "Our Stars," and although the title seemed fairly benign, everyone knew that these kids did not participate in the mainstream classrooms of our local schools. Some were simply underachievers, others the products of difficult family situations or life circumstances. Others had simply lost a sense of their own nature. Possibly, they were never fully accepted and searched for someplace that might include them. As a local educator described it to me, this community's after-school tutorial was the place of last resort, and many times was unknowingly marginalized by the establishment. These kids, who mostly wanted to be accepted, often found themselves more ostracized than ever.

My wife consistently says there are no bad kids, just kids who make bad choices. She preaches that most bad choices emerge from exhaustion or frustration from being unable to locate real significance or meaning in one's life. Come to think of it, I know a lot of adults who should probably be in some Life After-School Tutorial. My wife, who is a professor of education at a local college, explains that these kids seek something to fill missing pieces of their lives, but usually confront either their own limitations or others' unrealistic expectations. Most adults do not deal very well with rejection, failure, or disappointment; how can we expect kids to do any better? Faced with such obstacles, most of these kids resign themselves to the lowest of self-esteem and expectation and, ultimately, set themselves against the world.

There are exceptions, of course, but many times, it is either the result of chance or the heart of a caring individual who has decided not to give up on what can be in each of these children. As I watched the yellow school bus move down the parade route with the kids smiling and throwing candy out the windows, it struck me that someone had decided that there was something valuable and significant in each of these little ones, in spite of what had brought them to this program. It struck me that these kids did not seem like misfits or troublemakers as they laughed and shouted, "Merry Christmas!" Each child's name was written in glitter on a homemade star. They were having a good time and enjoying the moment. It struck me that if you had taken the sign off the side of the bus, no one along that route would have known that these children were different from other children. It struck me that these kids, who had been known for doing everything to challenge the rules of order, appeared happy, content, and at home with just being in the parade.

At this, my wife, seeing the tears in my eyes and sensing what I was thinking, turned to me and said, "Do you realize that this may be the most significant moment, thus far, in their lives?" A big softie, I struggled to reply without blubbering, but finally was able to mutter, "Yes." For most of the parade's participants, this was one of many opportunities to walk down the street singing, laughing, and being part of the excitement. But for these kids in the yellow school bus, the parade gave them a chance to shine and, for a short period, to be known simply as part of a moment's joy. I was pleased and humbled by what I saw, but I was also saddened, knowing that God unveils significance in front of me every day. I would see it more often if I would just stop and watch life through the eyes of the meek of this world.

The Meaning of *Significant*

Not long ago, I was asked to make a presentation to a group of Christian business leaders concerning spirituality's impact on organizational leadership. The topic of the seminar was "Spirituality in the

Boardroom: The Role of Faith in Building the Significant Organization." My task was to talk about the personal spiritual values that Christian business leaders should exhibit when leading their respective organizations. For days, I batted around one idea after another, only to find myself re-creating the same presentation I had heard again and again about success or achievement. After some time, though, I began to focus less on faith and leadership and more on the word *significant*.

I only thought I understood the word. For me, *significant* had always meant "large." Thus, my notion of building a significant organization immediately connected to a large institutional structure whether in terms of sales, staffing, or global impact. However, as I discovered, the definition of *significant* is more complex.

Take a look at how *Webster's* defines the word: "sig·nif·i·cant: adj 1: important in effect or meaning; 2: fairly large; 3: too closely correlated to be attributed to chance and therefore indicating a systematic relation; 4: rich in significance or implication."[7] The word actually has four different meanings associated with it. First, it suggests something that has value. Second, *significant* indicates that which is noticeable and measurable. Third, *significant* things derive from focus and purpose and not from mere chance. And finally, *significant* implies an effect on its surroundings.

I realized that the *significant* organization must first exhibit basic, foundational qualities before providing *substantial results*. In a results-oriented society, a primary and oftentimes rudimentary step is missed by not focusing first on the values that shape both our reason to produce and the means by which we accomplish results. The same can be said for life in general. Although our world has been inundated with self-help books and programs, what matters is the innermost part of our souls that says *why* we produce is as important as *what* we produce. The *significant* life is not defined simply by the results, but by the process. Thus, the most *significant* life may not be the most famous or wealthy person, but the one who has simply lived life well.

Long after the presentation was over, I continued to think of those around me who had lived significant lives by staying true to their basic principles, oftentimes in spite of incredible odds. What emerged was a list of some of the most important people in my life and their litany of values that had shaped my own path. And I realized, like the forming of creation itself, these values resonated from a common thread of faith born through the life of God.

If we are to live significant lives, we must first be willing to cling to the value of life itself. Too often, Christians reduce our time on this earth to a stopover on the way to some eternal resort. On the contrary, the significant life realizes the gift of this journey and, in spite of its difficulties, treasures the moments, good and bad, as opportunities to experience and share a unique and profound joy.

During the final days of my grandmother's life as she battled cancer, she fought tooth and nail for each breath. Many in the family could not understand why she held on so long, but I came to understand her struggle. With all of its sadness and disappointment, she had also seen great joy in her life. Although she was more than convinced of her eternal future, my grandmother cherished the unique beauty this world had to offer. And, when she died, the testimony of her life was marked by a witness born out through the lives she touched. At the wake, one person after another told how my grandmother's zest for life and impenetrable hope had changed the way they assessed their own journeys. They knew her life had not been easy, but she had made a concerted effort not to allow difficulties to define her, and in the end, her effect on those around her was more than *significant*. The mark of the significant life, even in one as meek as my grandmother, is measured not in its possessions or position, but in its value and effect on others. The saddest, most insignificant lives are those in which persons have resigned themselves to the motion of living without the meaning of living. They appear to be functional and successful in light of the world's expectations, yet they miss what has real value.

One Significant Step After Another

"My name is Lonny," said the large man sitting at the end of the table. He did not get up, but reached across the table to shake my hand. As we went around with introductions of those at the table, we were to tell our names and something unique about ourselves. "I am a football coach," Lonny said, after joking about having trouble finding anything unique to say about his life.

He looked like a football coach. A big man with huge, broad shoulders, Lonny resembled a linebacker. Another noticeable trait was Lonny's huge, weathered hands. I could only imagine them flailing through the air while shouting commands and calling plays. All the stereotypes of coaches flashed in my mind. But it didn't take long to realize that Lonny's personality differed from the usual macho demeanor. Although I am sure that he definitely could scare any teenage misfit, he was gentle and extremely attentive.

I spent most of the evening making small talk with those around the table, but I connected to Lonny more than anyone else that night. I found him to be a truly honest, joyful person who seemed to appreciate every moment. His laughter revealed that he loved people and, I believed, genuinely wished for others to do so as well. He spoke with carefully chosen words and seemed shy with language and expressions.

As the meeting ended, people made their way from their seats, offering "good-byes" to each other before leaving the restaurant for their cars. I noticed that Lonny seemed to limp, but I chalked it up to an exhausting day of coaching or some recurring ache, the result of a long ago football injury. Little did I know.

I would see Lonny several times over the next weeks as we prepared for the launch of the new church's first worship service. Each time, he wore the same ensemble—sweatpants, T-shirt, and a ball cap. I would not have thought much about it except sweatpants seemed inappropriate in the middle of June in South Mississippi, and I noticed that Lonny also walked with a deliberate, carefully placed stride. On one afternoon, while unloading furniture in the newly rented church office, Lonny complained of a blister on his right leg. He sat down on a load of boxes and proceeded to remove his leg from the knee down. I had no idea and, at the time, felt more than a little embarrassed. He looked at the red, scarred stump just below his knee and then reattached the prosthetic. Then to my further amazement, he did the same with the other leg.

Looking up, Lonny could tell by the expression on my face that I had not realized his situation. At first he grinned and then it turned into a full-blown cackle as he informed everyone of my bewilderment. My mind kept going back to that first conversation around the table when Lonny struggled to come up with something unique about himself. As I would learn later, to Lonny, the prostheses were not unique; they were simply a part of him, a detachable part mind you, but not a part he felt needed to be explained.

As the story was recollected to me, it was a normal night during his freshman year of college that changed Lonny's life forever. While walking a friend home from a local party, Lonny and the friend were hit at a crosswalk by a drunk driver. Lonny says the pain is the only real memory of the tragic event; the details are sketchy. He remembers stepping out into the street and then little after that. But he does remember the pain. He also remembers wondering about his friend. Lonny learned later that she was killed on impact.

Lonny experienced months of surgery, rehabilitation, and setbacks before he left the hospital. The doctors were unable to save either of his mangled legs, and eventually, both were amputated below the knee. All the promise that a tough, good-looking college freshman could imagine was shattered in the blink of an eye. Ironically, the driver of the car turned out to be a local football star.

Over the next years, Lonny carefully reassembled his life. He married and became the father of four. In addition to being a football coach, he is a teacher at a local high school, where thousands of young people have been touched by his story and by his courage in the face of his disability. However, Lonny's most profound example is found in the everyday normality of his life. First, he is a husband and a father. He faces the same day-to-day struggles of anyone trying to raise a family in our modern culture. Second, he is a community volunteer, extremely active in everything from his church to the fight against cancer. Third, he is a devoted teacher and mentor to countless young people. But more than anything, Lonny is a devoted child of God. Once asked how he is able to appear so normal in the face of such overwhelming obstacles, Lonny replied, "Everyone faces obstacles; mine are just more noticeable to the naked eye."

Many look at Lonny and feel pity. But the primary emotion that should ignite in each of us is recognition. As we experience our own limps in this imperfect world, we are called to live beyond the disabilities and disappointments. For many, it is much easier to notice Lonny's disability than it is to realize our own more personal, intrinsic struggles, many times associated with the less noticeable, disabling traits of an aimless, purposeless existence.

What keeps Lonny going? Deep core values about life, family, love, and forgiveness. When times are bad, Lonny uses these simple principles to provide an emotional life preserver that holds him until the storm passes. In the good times, Lonny does not abandon these basic truths. He uses them to live out his full potential as a humble, faithful brother in Christ. The core of these beliefs may seem simple to the watching world, even meek perhaps, but their power is unmistakable. To that end, for me and many others, Lonny lives one of the most *significant* lives in God's creation. And, he is a magnificent spiritual hero.

Exceptionally Simple Significance

The third blessing is about the meek of this world who actually turn out to be heirs to the throne. The meek of whom Jesus speaks are not famous or renowned by the world's standards, but they weave threads into the basic fabric of their surroundings in such notable ways that those with whom they come into contact are the better for it. But shouldn't that be the real nature of anyone's life? Not so much to be recognized by the world, but by another person's soul, much the way those on a ship might see a lighthouse?

Jesus flips the meaning of *significant* and *meek* in reference to how the world defines them. Like the looking glass in *Alice in Wonderland*, Jesus refashions our spiritual senses, which appear awkward and undone to the human eye, but ultimately are refreshing and convincing to our souls. The disciples certainly did not understand fully what he was trying to convey; however, there must have been an incredible sense of possibility among them, even in the midst of their confusion. The spiritual message of the day had too long become jaded and rigid, excluding the very ones for whom God cared most. Jesus instructed that all of this was changed; that the destitute are kings, the mourners are joyful, and the meek are heirs. What nonsense it must have seemed! But, oh, how sweet it must have sounded. Certainly, Jesus had come to complete the law, but not as they had expected.

It was a shocking message to everyone but those who had paid attention to Jesus from the beginning. His words made no secret of where his message derived or where it led, and for this, Jesus' blessings made him dangerous. On the surface, he may have seemed meek. Kings are not born in stables; warriors do not battle with ideas and love; revolutionaries do not preach peace. But his words spoke deeply, and he knew that if you gave the downtrodden hope, you gave them purpose. Give them purpose, and they could change the world. One has to look only at Gandhi or Martin Luther King Jr. to understand the power of hope—for in the power of hope, the meek become significant.

If it had not been for Josephus or Tacitus, there might have been no worldly or historical reference to this man from Nazareth. But we would certainly have known of him, just the same. For the impact that Jesus made on the world came not from history books or grand accomplishments, or from civilizations conquered or kingdoms transformed, but from the testimonies of men and women who were changed by his teachings. In just three years, through only a handful of believers, over a geography smaller than the state of Rhode Island, this teacher, rabbi, and friend changed the world. No swords, shields, uprisings, or sieges, just a basic, humble life *lived well* in relationship with God, according to God's way of life.

The prospect of humble lives lived well that have the power to change the world is both intriguing and hopeful. It is intriguing because it debunks the insistence of our modern culture that significance rests only with the powerful. Jesus clearly rejects this and calls the meek the inheritors of creation. For as Jesus insists, the meek understand the delicate balance between need and want; abundance and poverty. Any of us, regardless of status or position, possess the promise of God's blessing and the eternal potential as God's children. Jesus teaches many times throughout his ministry that our lives may face hardship, disappointment, and obstacles, but our song of hope is not of this world alone. It stretches beyond our mortal bonds and rings forever in God's heart. It echoes God's own special melody, and in this, we are blessed.

Notes

1. Brennan Manning, *The Ragamuffin Gospel* (Sisters, Ore.: Multnomah Publishers, 2000), 25.

2. *New York Times,* obituary page, May 28, 2005.

3. *New York Times,* obituary page, May 31, 2005.

4. *New York Times,* obituary page, May 31, 2005.

5. William Barclay, *The Gospel of Matthew,* vol. 1 (Louisville: Westminster John Knox Press, 2001), 111-12.

6. *Interpreter's Commentary,* 282-83.

7. Merriam-Webster's Online Dictionary.

The Fourth Blessing
The Heart That Craves for God

Blessed are those who hunger and thirst for righteousness,
for they will be filled.
—*Matthew 5:6*

Now we understand that the blanket really does protect
Linus and that Schroeder really does play lovely music on
a toy piano, because both of them keep at it. They believe.
—*Anne Lamott*[1]

How Much Do You Want Righteousness?

I have an uncle who used to say, "Son, if you have a choice between marrying a woman who is beautiful or marrying a woman who is a good cook, always choose the good cook—beauty fades, but the kitchen will always be open." Come to think of it, this uncle died a bachelor.

Regardless, I never had to choose. My wife is a gorgeous woman and a good cook—a cross between supermodel Cindy Crawford and gourmet chef Julia Child. This is not to say that she always enjoys cooking. We spend our fair share eating out. However, this has more to do with schedules and professional lives than ability or desire. In fact, there is no more wonderful sight or smell than working side by side with my wife in the kitchen on some new creation or favorite dish.

My favorites are her homemade spaghetti and meat sauce and her homemade chicken noodle soup. Once the food is ready and the table is set, the Stanford Five sit and enjoy a great time of good food and stimulating conversation, even though, many times, it is conducted in a third grade and kindergarten vernacular. And, I am not shy about enjoying the meal, for I do not eat just one serving; I eat three. Although I stand only five feet eight inches tall and weigh barely 150 pounds, my wife says that I eat enough for three grown men.

However, the best part happens several hours later. As much as I enjoy the meal and the family sitting around the table, I am all the more notorious for late-night snacking. It is not uncommon to find me some-time around midnight warming up leftovers of the previous night's din-ner. The scene always plays the same. My wife will stagger, half asleep, into the kitchen after having heard some noise, only to discover me standing, fork drawn, over the food. "What are you doing?" she used to ask. "I am eating leftovers," I would reply. "You ate three plates at din-ner," she would always say. "But I am hungry" would be my consistent retort. *Gluttony* might be a better way to describe it. I can't remember ever being truly hungry. Sure, there have been times when I wanted food or, at least, more food. Goodness knows that no one can enjoy a Yoo-hoo or a Snickers better than I. But to say that I have been hungry would be far from the truth. For most of us, hunger and thirst relate only to breaks in our day when we have not had the appropriate meal or snack in a cer-tain number of hours. Many of us have spoken the words, "I am hungry," or "I am thirsty," only to intend that we have not had our "fill." But this was not the case in Jesus' day. As he shares this fourth beatitude, his lis-teners understand the real nature of hunger and thirst, and they do not take it lightly.

For many, food was minimal at best, with feasts or eating to one's fill reserved for special or rare occasions. Most people in Jesus' day ate meat only once per week, and that was reserved for those with steady, affluent lifestyles. Thus, meals were a privilege, as much ritual and rite of cele-bration as the consumption of food. People knew real hunger in Jesus' day, and even for the most well-to-do, people saw, felt, and lived the effects of real poverty and deficiency. All working, middle-class people in Palestine knew they were only a meal or so from starvation. The hunger of which Jesus spoke related not to a missed lunch or snack, but to a painful longing for nourishment, and if this condition was not addressed, they would die.[2]

However, as real as hunger was in Jesus' day, thirst was even more pro-found. The climate and oftentimes shifting conditions of the Palestinian desert provided every inhabitant with a parched, dry thirst that could become unbearable. Water was valuable and required effort to obtain. The thirst of which Jesus spoke was not quenched by a trip through Starbucks or to the local vending machine, but it was an all-consuming desire for water, without which they could not go on.[3]

My wife may ask, "What are you hungry for?" when asking about our evening dinner plans. But my response is about choice, picking from a menu of plenty instead of responding to the dark reality of scarcity. I might reply, "Chicken sounds good or how about something with pasta," but the scene is usually tempered by the reality of a hearty lunch or adequate breakfast, buffered by plenty of snacking along the way. My wife's question is not dire. Its answer does not presume that my hunger, if gone unchecked, will ultimately kill me. No, McDonald's and KFC would not hear of it.

Most of us in modern American culture have no real equivalent for life-threatening hunger or thirst. Unless we are among the marginalized, poor, or homeless in our communities, we may not fully understand the depth of the needs to which Jesus referred.

The image Jesus casts of hunger and thirst was stark, edgy, and uncomfortable. His words were not meant to make us feel good about ourselves, but to push us, bully us if you will, into thinking about the real nature of what we crave in this world. People who know real hunger see the question, "What are you hungry for?" in a different light. They know that this kind of hunger and yearning will have far-reaching, powerful implications.

Jesus paints the yearning for righteousness with images of intense hunger and thirst. The Greek word that is translated "righteousness" is *dikaiosune*, which essentially means living God's way. It means thinking, feeling, and acting in daily life with justice, integrity, and a sense of virtue, all of which emerge from a right relationship with God. Hunger and thirst were not associated with choosing food and drink from a buffet of plenty. The verbs express a desire so pervasive that nothing else will do. The people of Jesus' day knew that real hunger and thirst drove a person to the point of self-sacrifice and denial. Jesus might ask, "Does our search for righteousness create in us the same desire?" "Do we really crave righteousness more than anything else in this world?" "Are we willing to pay the price that such cravings require?" The fourth blessing hits at people's real desire for righteousness—encouraging their efforts to be more than wistful, meaningless offerings, but a real, intense yearning that can potentially transform their worlds.

"You say you want righteousness," Jesus asks, "but do you want righteousness like a person who is starving wants food?" Not mincing words, Jesus hits right at the heart. However, he goes deeper: "You say you want righteousness, but do you want righteousness like a person dying of thirst wants water?" Jesus knew that our tone would change against the backdrop of such questioning. Jesus' understanding of hunger and thirst points to the core of our deepest worldly feelings and emotions and asks the most disturbing of questions, "So, in light of this kind of hunger and thirst for earthly things, how do your spiritual cravings look? How much do you really crave living God's way?"

Sam and Gayle

"Life is not fair, but you knew that," I said to Sam as he stood looking at the ground, hands in his pockets. It was not the answer he wanted, but one he was expecting and with which he was familiar. In his late thirties, Sam was a licensed practicing counselor turned pastor. No one knew more about life's imperfections than he did. I had known Sam since I attended graduate school. We became friends during a fire drill at a local hospital. He had been visiting his ailing grandmother while I was finishing work for a pastoral care class. As the sirens wailed, the hospital went into a lock-down mode as security herded all nonessential personnel through underground corridors, lit with a dull, translucent, emergency red. Finally, we exited into the courtyard of the hospital's outside gardens and waited for the drill to end.

I knew from the beginning that Sam was extremely bright and that he had a heart for God. He spoke with crisp tones that had a serious edge, much too serious for someone his age at the time. He also had a gentle nature and a subtle and cutting wit once you got to know him. It was easy to like Sam and even easier to talk to him. Some people just have the gift of listening. Sam never particularly liked this special talent, but he realized that God had placed within him whatever it was that made people feel comfortable as they talked about their deepest fears and hurts. And Sam's responses were always dead-on with a genuine care for the person and an unusual wisdom for someone so young. Place these together, and Sam was frequently sought out to listen to people's problems. In fact, this dynamic introduced Sam to his future wife. Sam met Gayle while he was working as an intern at an on-campus counseling clinic. Gayle walked through the door and changed Sam's life forever.

She worked as a hospitality usher for the college and was responsible for escorting various recruits and their families on tours of the campus. The Counseling Center was always Gayle's favorite because of, she would later say, the interesting folks she met on each visit. On one such tour, Gayle met Sam, who was physically sitting on one of the clients in the floor of the center's entrance. The client, who it was later discovered suffered from paranoid delusions, pulled a knife on the receptionist after being told that he would have to come back since he did not have an appointment. Moments before Gayle and the VIPs arrived, Sam approached the man from behind and administered the only restraining hold he knew, one he had learned no less from watching wrestling matches as a child. Only problem was that Sam knew no other such moves and resorted to sitting on the guy until authorities arrived. Over the years, Sam and Gayle would tell this story many times with Gayle always joking that Sam didn't even "stand up to shake her hand." "Nevertheless," she would continue, "he made quite a first impression— albeit sitting down." However, after meeting Sam, her visits to the Counseling Center became even more frequent because, according to her own admission, she had met the most interesting character of all.

To say that Gayle was beautiful was an understatement. She had every feature that makes for an attractive person, including a stunning smile and unbelievable eyes. Everyone admitted it, men and women alike. Throughout her life, Gayle walked into just about every room knowing that most, if not all, eyes were on her. Most of us dream of such a "burden," but for Gayle, it masked a deeper need for affection and affirmation. Add to the equation a mother whose attention swung from absent to overbearing within moments and a distant, removed father, and one quickly found a wounded soul behind Gayle's beautiful face. With her looks and engaging personality, Gayle, as I would later discover, tried to fill the void in her life by engaging in a pattern of intense, but shallow relationships that did little for her soul or her reputation.

Few matchmakers would have put Sam and Gayle together. Sam was not, as people say, a "looker." Barely five feet ten inches tall, Sam, unlike Gayle, did not turn heads when he walked in a room. His physical stature was modest and unassuming. Combined with Sam's oftentimes serious nature were graying hair and a receding hairline, creating the impression that Sam was much older. I remember this distinctly from one of their Christmas cards several years later, commenting to myself how this couple seemed very "May-December" or at least "August."

As my wife and I would discuss Sam and Gayle over the years, she would say that Sam was not unattractive but "under the radar." His real charm lay more in his sense of humor, kindness, and attitude—and especially in the fact that when you talked to him, he always looked intently into your eyes. Thus, the bond between Sam and Gayle had less to do with physical attraction, disturbing most of the world's expectations, and more to do with what I call "fit"—that quality in relationships where totally opposite personalities find real connection through more emotional, intellectual, or spiritual qualities. My wife and I have this, and so do Sam and Gayle.

Gayle brought out the energy and daredevil in Sam. Her zest for life always challenged his calm nature. She was never on time; Sam was never late. Gayle loved parties; Sam preferred more private gatherings. Gayle wanted spontaneity; Sam liked order and a plan. But Sam filled the lonely places in Gayle and gave her a sense of security that no one in her life had managed to do. When you saw them together, talking and looking at each other, you sensed their relationship was deeper than love; it was inspiration. Many a time, at some social event, I would catch Sam and Gayle sitting together in a chair or on a sofa, with her head gently resting against his. There seemed no more natural picture.

However, Sam and Gayle were alike in two ways. Both possessed keen intellect and ambition, especially related to their careers. Gayle was the youngest member of her law school class and was immediately hired by a topnotch firm on the East Coast. Sam moved his practice to suit her new job situation, all the while becoming, in his own right, noted as one of the best counselors in the area. Adept at meeting people where they were, Sam found himself swamped by clients from all walks of life. Although his work was beneficial, it was also draining and filled with every sort of problem imaginable. Sam's nature craved helping people, but the various interactions were taking a toll.

Finally, Sam literally grew tired of counseling. It wasn't necessarily the clients as much as their various struggles, mistakes, and trials, coupled with the clients' inability to develop the faintest idea of what had brought them to such a place or the real desire necessary to rectify the problem. So, just five years into his practice, Sam enrolled in school again and earned his Master of Divinity. Immediately, his denomination offered him a position in a large, urban congregation not far from Gayle's law practice. Sam was hired as a teaching pastor and quickly began serving as staff and congregational counselor. He became known for his ability to listen and provide guidance. But, over the ensuing years, Sam and Gayle found themselves drifting more toward the affirmation and responsibilities of their vocations instead of each other, which is a recipe for disaster in any marriage.

When I met Sam twelve years earlier, he was engaged to Gayle. They married several years later in a modest, beautiful ceremony in the small town where his parents lived. The wedding was simple and elegant. In many ways, it was a perfect day. You could see the hope in their eyes as they smiled and laughed together. Truly, they looked like best friends and soul mates. And yet, even then, I saw a tension in their relationship, not so much between them as between the circumstances of families and expectations. No matter how independent Gayle wanted to be, it was evident that shaking the bonds of an obviously enmeshed family system was more than just difficult; it was overwhelming. And Sam's need to fix everyone, even when he had not chosen to do so, could be volatile and draining. I remember thinking how delicate this formula seemed, especially for two people so driven and in such demand by the relationships of this world.

And, so, as we stood under the same large oak tree in the hospital courtyard where we first met, little was different with our friendship, save the normal life changes that happen with time's passage, yet much was not right in other places.

"Fair?" Sam said to me, his tone shifting with his usual carefully chosen words and emotions nowhere in sight. "She had an affair, Shane. She didn't wreck the car or forget a birthday!" Sam's eyes narrowed, his voice becoming dry and quiet, "I don't think 'fair' quite covers it."

Several weeks earlier, Gayle had admitted to an affair with one of her law partners. It had been over for some time, but the emotion and details were painful. Throughout the two-year period in question, Sam and

Gayle's marriage was strained immensely. Their vocations had led them down separate roads, and although this particular transgression was Gayle's, the blame belonged to both.

Sam thought the pastorate would ease their marriage. Instead, he traded the troubles of people who at least made appointments and worked within certain office hours, for others who believed the pastor was on call twenty-four hours a day. By the time everyone had been tended to, Sam had very little left to share with Gayle, and her need for affirmation eventually pushed her to discover attention elsewhere.

"Can you think of a word that would cover it?" I asked Sam.

Sam turned abruptly, raising his voice, "How about *betrayal, low down, rotten*...?" Then he paused, the tears welling in his eyes as he peered up into the large oak tree. He said softly, "How about *unbelievable?*" Sam looked back at me and said, "I guess I just never thought she would do something like this—not to me." Gone was the harsh tone. Now, I was simply standing in front of a man who looked like and really was convinced that he had lost his best friend.

I motioned for us to sit on the bench perched beneath the oak. "Sam," I said, trying to think of what to say next, "why does Gayle think it happened?"

Sam looked down at the palms of his hands. "She says that I became distant and preoccupied with everyone and everything but her. She keeps saying that she tried to reach me, but when I couldn't...or wouldn't respond, someone else did."

"Is it true?" I asked.

"Yes, but people go through things like this all the time...you just don't cross some lines...," Sam said intently.

I interrupted, "Now, do you really think Gayle got up one morning and decided to cross the line, or do you think Satan kept inching that line close enough to her that it became too easy to fall across?"

"I can't believe you are taking her side," Sam said.

"Sam, I am not taking her side, but I know how confusing it gets when life's 'lines,' or whatever you want to call them, get redrawn around us," I said, putting my hand on his shoulder. "Look at me, Sam. The adversary is the master at taking our cravings and needs and then falsely convincing us that our appetites are more important than our virtues."

Sam looked at me, and I continued, "And he will use whatever is necessary to exploit those emotions and feelings whether it is our work, another person, or...," I slowed to make sure that he heard what I was about to say, "...even our pride. He is a lion, Sam, and all he wants is to destroy what means the most to us."

Sam looked at me, the knot in his throat tightening. "Sam, a wise friend once said that sometimes in life, things happen and you simply must walk away, but other times, you put your best wrestling move on them and hold on for dear life." For the first time in the conversation, I saw a smile as Sam recognized his own words.

"What does Gayle want?" I asked Sam.

"She says that she wants me, and that for the first time in her life she knows clearly what is important and what she really needs," Sam said.

"What do you want?" I asked.

"Shane, I know where this is going...," Sam said, resistance evident in his tone.

I interrupted, pointedly asking, "Sam, what do you want?"

He continued, "I don't think I can live with this, the images, feelings..."

"Sam, this is not a question of what you can live *with*; it is a question of what you can't live *without*."

He grew quiet, and I knew that I had his attention. "Even a broken heart can be healed as long as it has a reason to beat, Sam."

Sam and I sat for several moments without saying a word. Eventually, I asked if I could pray with him, and he agreed. After the prayer, I told him that I would check later to see how he was doing, but that he should not hesitate to call if he needed me.

"I know what I need," he said.

As I walked away, Sam pulled out his cell phone and dialed a familiar number. "Honey...," I heard him say.

Knowing What We Need

The fourth blessing is demanding and difficult to hear. Jesus wants us to do more than hear its meaning; he wants us to feel, almost physically, its power. Nowhere is this more evident than in the grammar of the language itself. Barclay suggests that in the Greek, whenever the word for hunger or thirst is used, it is often followed by the genitive case. For example, if someone were to hunger for bread, the actual translation would be "hunger for some of the bread," not the whole loaf. The same is true for thirst. The Greek would also translate that a thirsty person wanted "some water," not the entire bucket.[4]

However, in this passage, Jesus says, "Blessed are those who hunger and thirst for righteousness." The word for righteousness is in the accusative tone, meaning that Jesus wants us to hunger and thirst, not for a part of righteousness, but for all of it. It is not an option to live *with* righteousness along with other priorities. No, it becomes the all-consuming nature of existence and something without which we cannot survive.[5]

And yet, we should not miss that nowhere does Jesus say blessed are those who *have* complete righteousness. The blessing goes to those who crave it. Whether we possess it fully seems left to the divine grace and plan of God.[6]

One Wyoming Woman

A pastor tells the story of a young woman who called his office several weeks after Hurricane Katrina ravaged their coastal Mississippi community. She was a mom of three from the suburbs of a Western state, and had followed news of the disaster for several days. The woman, who was only marginally involved in her church, attended a local women's Bible study class, who had chosen to pray at each meeting for the victims of the hurricane. Through several days of prayer, the woman decided to help with the relief efforts.

After an Internet search revealed the name of the pastor's small town, the woman called his office asking what procedures would need to be in place for her to bring a work team to the area to help. Through a lengthy conversation, the pastor informed the woman of the process and then asked how many people she had on her team. The woman replied, "Oh, it's only me right now, but I know God will provide others."

The pastor, who had become quite polished in dealing with various good-hearted people who had no real means or intentions to actually bring teams, convinced the young woman to pray for her plans until God provided the necessary workers. He believed, as he had learned with so many others, that he would probably never hear from her again. He was wrong.

The young woman called every day for three weeks with updates on supplies, contributions, and, yes, the team member search. Team member number two joined on Day Eight; number three on Day Sixteen. A date was set for late November for the work team to arrive on a Saturday and to return home ten days later.

The Tuesday prior to the departure date, the young woman called to give a final update on the team's status, complete with travel arrangements and transportation to the airport. Finally, the pastor asked, "How many team members do you have now?"

"Still three," the woman answered, "but I know that God will provide more." The pastor was taken aback by her answer. He had learned over the weeks following the disaster that it took ten to twelve members of a well-organized team to be truly effective, and this was the minimum. Any smaller and the team became more of a hindrance than a help.

This particular pastor had learned to be resourceful and optimistic, but even for him, this mission team project sounded doubtful, almost impossible.

"Why don't you call me on Thursday with another update?" the pastor insisted, trying to think of how he could talk her out of coming between now and then.

"Sure," she said, oblivious to the pastor's real motive, and after the usual pleasantries, they hung up.

The pastor spent the next forty-eight hours creating every excuse in the book for why this mission team should not happen. He had grown to like the young woman's tenacity and faith and did not want to crush her optimism, but he also wanted to be truthful and realistic. The last thing he or his congregation needed during this difficult time was to expend efforts that would provide little in the way of constructive work. If nothing else, disasters streamline what is considered useful and what is not.

The woman called promptly at 10:00 a.m. on Thursday. Preparing to give her the "you just don't have enough people to come" speech, he was startled by the excitement in her voice.

"Eighteen," she said, almost yelling into the phone. "We have eighteen people!"

At first, the pastor thought that he had heard wrong or that the stress had finally gotten to the young woman. Certainly, she did not say *eighteen*.

"How many?" he asked.

"Eighteen! God has given us fifteen more people since Tuesday!" she replied. And then with a chuckle in her voice, she finished by saying, "Pastor, I told you God would provide others."

"Yes, you did," the pastor said, laughing through the shock. "Yes, you did."

Three days later, eighteen people arrived at the airport ready to serve and help. As they lived and worked in the pastor's small, ravaged town, alongside others from the community and around the country, people witnessed a group of committed brothers and sisters whose hearts and hands showed the love of Jesus. Their work was effective, and their enthusiasm, driven by the young woman who had formed and led them, was much needed and appreciated. Many still remark that, of all the teams, this young woman's group of eighteen had more fire, faith, and fun than any.

At the end of the ten days, the young woman's team prepared to leave. In just a short time, they had not only formed bonds with one another, but had become members of the community as well. It was a sad good-bye, but with evidence of amazing grace and care.

Just before getting in the van to go to the airport, the young woman pulled the pastor aside and said quietly, "Please pray for one other thing. . . . All of the team members paid their entire expenses to make the trip, and most of them could not afford it. I am praying that God will provide some contributions when I return home so that I can give them a small portion of their money back."

The trip had indeed been expensive, and it would take a significant amount of money to return even a small portion of the cost.

"How much do you have raised so far?" the pastor asked.

"None," the woman replied and with a smile began to say, "but God..."

The pastor interrupted her: "I know. But God will provide." The woman laughed, hugged her newfound friend, and stepped into the van. The pastor no longer doubted the faith of this woman. He had never met anyone who so loved doing good but, more than anything, who so trusted God.

Several days later, the young woman called. After a few moments of discussing the work sites and the community, the pastor asked, "Oh, how are your contributions going?"

The woman's answer was like a burst of energy. "You won't believe it!" she said. "God provided enough to refund every team member 100 percent!" Then she finished, "The trip didn't cost them anything but faith!"

The pastor replied, "That is wonderful, but you are wrong on one count."

"What's that?" she asked.

"After meeting y'all and watching God work through you, I do believe it. Trust me, I believe it."

The pastor shared this story several months later. When asked what he believed was the key to this woman's unwavering faith and success, and after a few moments with a sly smile on his face, he replied, "It was a good and right thing to do, and she craved it!"

Built to Crave

We are built to crave. It is as powerful and volatile a part of our nature as any other attribute. When we crave wrong, unhealthy things, the results can be devastating. For instance, I have watched people who have craved unhealthy relationships become spiritually anemic or anesthetized by the process. Their hearts harden under the guilt and shame of not seeking what is right. After enough time, the lie turns in on them until not only are they incapable of telling others the truth, but they cannot identify it for themselves. When they do finally confront the truth, the results are extremely painful and can have long-term ramifications for their most dear and sacred relationships, and for their inner, spiritual health. Although redemption and restoration are always possible, the road is often long and challenging. Throughout my ministry, this was always the most difficult journey to watch.

When we crave God's things, things like righteousness, justice, and love, the potential for good is just as powerful. The Bible says God does not withhold what is right and good from God's children. When we "seek first the kingdom," the Scripture promises that we have an abundance, maybe not of the world's fare, but of all that we truly need

(Matthew 6:33 NKJV). The voids and insecurities that propel us into so many bad decisions are replaced with hope, affirmation, and peace born through the love of God in Christ Jesus, but not just in rhetoric. Christ put his life on the line for this promise; therefore, it is not empty nor will it fail. There are no cul-de-sacs, no matter how well organized, in God's kingdom, only straight paths that, when taken, make for a marvelous, hopeful journey that sustains us and fills our souls with righteousness beyond what we could ever imagine.

Notes

1. Anne Lamott, *Traveling Mercies: Some Thoughts on Faith* (New York: Anchor Books, 1999), 189.

2. William Barclay, *The Gospel of Matthew*, vol. 1 (Louisville: Westminster John Knox Press, 2001), 114.

3. Ibid., 114-15.

4. Ibid., 116-17.

5. Ibid., 117.

6. *Interpreter's Commentary*, 283.

The Fifth Blessing
Doing Life Together

Blessed are the merciful, for they will receive mercy.
—Matthew 5:7

Many people mistake our work for our vocation. Our vocation is the love of Jesus.
—Mother Teresa[1]

Glorified Tissue Dispenser

While walking to my car after a breakfast meeting on a recent business trip, I noticed a woman crying as she was sitting in the driver's seat of her car. The intensity of her sobbing indicated that she was very upset. I passed by, not wanting to intrude, though I felt the impulse to respond in some way. Honestly, I was more than a little curious about her situation, wondering what could have upset her so.

After briefly reflecting on the moment, I turned around, walked back to her car window, and gently knocked on the glass. "Ma'am, are you okay?" I asked, knowing full well that she was not. It did run through my mind, just after asking it, that the question seemed useless. I asked it anyway, as I'm sure many of us do when we cannot think of something better.

The woman seemed also to realize the absurdity of my question, pausing to look at me with that "if I were okay, I wouldn't be sitting here crying" look. Yet she was gracious and simply answered, "Yes, I'm fine." Both of us knew she was certainly not fine, but we were simply asking and answering in the vein of cordial, polite conversation in our culture.

"Can I do anything to help?" I asked this time. This seemed like a better question. It showed that I didn't believe she was actually okay and that her response was out of habit or courtesy.

She smiled slightly and responded, "No, I'm fine."

At this point, I should have followed up with something more profound, but all I mustered was, "Well, I hope your day gets better," once again testifying that what we were saying to each other and what we were seeing did not match. Trying to appear helpful, I took out a tissue from my pocket and handed it to the woman. "You look like you might need this," I said.

"Thank you," she said politely, offering a slight, but sweet smile. I smiled back, tapped the door gently, and walked away.

Later in the day, I recounted the story over dinner with my wife. I was proud of my interaction. I had seen a sister in need and had responded. I was also proud of not having been overbearing because I believe that all of us should have the freedom to deal with our difficulties in whatever way we choose, even though we may have to deal with them alone at times.

After I ended, my wife looked at me and said, "Did you ask if she wanted to talk or if she needed you to call anyone?"

"No," I replied, somewhat taken aback by her lack of praise. Feeling the need to go on the defensive, I blurted out, "But I asked if I could do anything to help."

"You didn't ask what was wrong?" my wife said, moving quickly past my retort.

I said no this time, replying with an attitude and a touch of moral indignation, really wanting to say, *I could have walked by and done nothing.*

"Let me get this straight," my wife said, looking at me with that look as only a spouse can, part sarcasm and part disbelief. "You approach an obviously upset woman sitting in a car, ask her a series of questions that any friend would hesitate to answer in such a condition, much less a stranger to a stranger, give her a tissue, and then walk away feeling as though you are Mother Teresa?"

Wow, I thought, sitting there in disbelief. This was most certainly not going in the direction I had hoped, and worse yet, my wife made sense. "Well, I . . . ," I stumbled through, trying to begin a sentence.

My wife placed her hand on mine and said, "So basically, honey, you were a glorified tissue dispenser. Doing the right thing, but for no good reason except the requirement of 'that's what good Christians do.'"

Tag! I hadn't been hit this hard since a fellow bus mate in the fifth grade took offense to my impression of his mother's new hairdo. All I wanted to do was the good Christian thing.

"I don't mean to hurt your feelings," my wife said.

Well, you did was my first thought, but I responded, "Oh, no, I understand," which, of course, I didn't, at least at that moment.

"Are you mad?" she continued.

"Of course not," I responded. *Liar!* my inner voice shouted. *You try to do the good Christian thing and this is how people see it,* my inner voice kept shouting and nagging. I hate that voice!

Deep down, though, I knew my wife was right. I had preached on this scenario many times, Christians feeling the need to do something but with no real intention or commitment to do what was necessary to actually help. Sure, there is validation in the response, a sense of pride, possibly even some kudos. But no matter how good I felt about what I had *done*, the mercy she needed never had time to sink in. At the end of it all, there remained a woman, sitting in her car, crying for some reason.

My wife looked at me and said, "Sweetheart, I know I am being hard on you, but you have told us in the congregation over and again that most times people don't need us to *do* anything. They just need us to *be* where they are."

"If you had been the woman in the car," I asked, "what would you have needed me to do?"

"I'm not sure," my wife replied. "Maybe just for you to offer that tissue, stand there a minute, and remind me that the front seat of my car is not the loneliest, scariest place in the world."

We smiled as she continued, "What is it that you like to say about moments like this?" I knew where she was going. "Take a moment to *be the tears...*," she said.

"And watch Jesus be the *comfort*" was my refrain, finishing the title of one of my own sermons.

Blessed Are the Courteous

I wish the fifth blessing read, "Blessed are the courteous, for they shall receive innumerable kudos from God." Unfortunately, this translation is nowhere to be found. The fifth blessing reads, "Blessed are the merciful, for they will receive mercy." As with the other blessings, our modern understanding of language pushes us to view mercy in only a twenty-first-century, Western framework. This is complicated by the fact that we live in a faith world that too often views Christian action alone as sufficient for Christian living and practice. No one understood this phenomenon better and worked to contradict it more than Mother Teresa. Her valiant efforts in reaching the most vulnerable of the world derived from a deeper understanding of mercy, sacrifice, and service. Mother Teresa once said that "many people mistake our work for our vocation. Our vocation is the love of Jesus."[2]

The fifth blessing is also not just admonishment for forgiveness. All of us know Jesus' words in the Lord's Prayer (asking God to "forgive us our trespasses, as we forgive those who trespass against us" [Matthew 6:9-15; Luke 11:2-4]). Although mercy instills a certain balance to forgiveness, encouraging us to make the act of forgiveness a real and central part of our hearts, forgiveness does not fully embrace the real nature of mercy as described by Jesus. For Jesus, mercy is a deeper, more personal experience that does not easily allow those involved to disconnect themselves. Mercy is spiritual glue.

The Greek word for merciful in this text is *eleemon*, which is similar in meaning to the Hebrew word *chesedh*. Whereas our modern reading of mercy stops with an action or feeling from one person to another, the Hebrew understanding of mercy literally means to get inside the life of another individual—to not only sympathize, as we understand the definition, with the other's perspective, but to experience it. Actually, this nuance is the appropriate reading of the Greek word for sympathy. *Sympathy* is the combination of two words: *syn*, which means to "join together with," and *paschein*, which means to "suffer or experience similar things." Put these together and the Greek meaning of *sympathy* was to literally "join in the suffering or experience of another person." No simple words or touch on the arm when responding to a person's need; this was a real-world, deep-in-the-heart, no-holds-barred kind of sympathy.[3]

However, this understanding of merciful speaks not only to our relationship with others, but also to the relationship that God has chosen to have with us. For example, *eleemon* is used in Hebrews 2:17 as a way of describing the nature of Christ's incarnation—the reason Jesus had to become like us in order to bring about the restoration of our souls and lives. The writer of Hebrews states that Christ became human in every way in order to fully understand the nature of our struggle and sin.

Through Christ's humanity, he became a "merciful [*eleemon*] and faithful High Priest before God" (v. 17, NLT). Jesus literally stepped into our experience, our shoes if you will, in order to share and display real mercy. Thus, as Jesus utters this fifth blessing, he is profoundly aware of what real mercy requires, but also of how important it is for our whole and complete salvation.[4]

The Bend of the River[5]

The Mississippi Delta has long been a place of stories. From the flat, fertile landscape to the striking culture and personalities, the Delta is a picture of the best and worst of humanity. Nowhere will you meet finer people and experience more unique places than in the Delta. However, the Delta also has a history of incredible injustice and inequality. It is a picture of contrasts—great wealth intertwined with immense poverty; great culture and refinement balanced by rampant illiteracy and social ills. These contrasts continue through generations of good, faithful, religious people. No matter the legislation or program, the Mississippi Delta is a living statement of such contrasts.

Thus, set against the backdrop of this world in the 1920s, the story of Elizabeth and Maxine becomes all the more remarkable. Elizabeth was the only daughter of one of the Delta's wealthiest men. A bank president and farmer, Elizabeth's father received the mantle of town leader from successive generations of his family ruling their small Delta community. Elizabeth grew up in a large antebellum home just north of town, a few hundred yards from the river's bend, a view that dominated anyone standing on the front porch of Elizabeth's home. Her world was filled with every luxury one could imagine, including a house full of servants and attendants. Although slavery had been outlawed for decades, the Mississippi Delta existed with a de facto class system whereby African Americans remained employed by the same families as their forefathers a hundred years before. Although "free," their lives still revolved around the plantation and around the families that had so dominated their pasts.

Elizabeth's father was a difficult, troubled man, especially with the sharecroppers and various employees. His temper could get the best of him, placing any number of people in harm's way. He believed in order and a distinctive hierarchy that prevented any interaction of the classes beyond the normal scope of one's job or position. Elizabeth saw this order lived out from her early childhood, and although her gentle spirit often felt otherwise, her standing as one of the community's first families prevented any digression.

Contrast Elizabeth's life with Maxine's. Maxine grew up in a sharecropper's shack located on land belonging to Elizabeth's family. The home sat nearly two miles from the plantation home, but ironically, it was on one of the higher spots in their Delta community. Thus, Maxine, too, was able to see the bend of the river, just as Elizabeth, though she saw it from a very different house. As far back as she knew, her family had worked this land, men and women toiling in the fields. Maxine's mother had been fortunate enough to earn a job working as a maid in the plantation's main home. For Maxine's family and for members of *her* community, this was a place of privilege, but only in terms of not having to work the fields. Maxine's mother's position afforded her a comfortable environment to be employed, but it was still a hard and oftentimes demeaning life. Even for the more privileged in Maxine's community, people struggled with poor living conditions and inadequate services such as public education, basic utilities, and health care.

Maxine's world of great want sat against Elizabeth's great abundance, and the two never crossed paths. Of course, the two girls knew each other and even played together when Maxine's mother brought her to work, but theirs was a world of great division and boundaries, and became increasingly so as they grew and took their places in their respective communities. Their friendship as children was tempered by unwritten, often unspoken understandings, of *how things had always been.* Although they lived cordial, courteous existences, and experienced much of their lives together, at the end of the day, they retreated to places far apart from each other, in theory at least, if not in miles.

When Maxine turned sixteen, she was offered a position working by her mother's side in the large plantation home. Schooling was limited for both girls. Maxine was expected to begin working, usually in the service of some wealthy family. Elizabeth was expected to marry a wealthy, capable man. This was especially important, given the fact that Elizabeth was an only child and, as believed in those days, would need a husband to help her run the family fortunes. Thus, several years after Maxine came to work as the maid of her childhood friend, she watched as Elizabeth married a promising young attorney named Thomas. Maxine would also marry about the same time to a mechanic named Robert, who was employed, you guessed it, by Elizabeth's father. However, unlike Elizabeth's world-class wedding that involved every well-to-do family within two hundred miles, Maxine and Robert married under an oak tree not far from her family's home and within sight of the river's bend.

Over the years, many things changed; but strangely, Elizabeth's and Maxine's lives ebbed with a sense of commonality and connection. Elizabeth's and Maxine's parents died within two years of one another. Elizabeth and Thomas became the possessors of great wealth in tangible things such as land and money, and in position. Maxine inherited her mother's position as the chief maid of the house and ran the home with such efficiency that all employees of the house and grounds answered to her first, before bothering Thomas or Elizabeth. Both couples had two children who lived past early childhood, and both lost children in childbirth. They saw the world pass before them in many of the same ways, again from different venues, and shared many of the same emotions of joy and sadness that this world brings. But no one ever confused their roles, and in spite of their common stories, they remained mistress of the house and servant. It was clear and tested, and neither violated its meaning.

Another common experience was their love for their husbands. Although hers was more an arranged marriage of convenience and possibility, Elizabeth had grown to love Thomas. His strong, reliant nature served their life and their relationship well. Their marriage actually grew stronger as the years passed. Maxine and Robert were no different. They found solace in each other's strong work habits and kind natures. They enjoyed their life together. Elizabeth and Maxine shared much in their lives—a land, a love of their children and husbands, a joy for life, and a view of the river to which both couples retreated in quiet moments.

Mark Twain said of the Mississippi River that "if this were some European river . . . it would be a holiday job . . . but this ain't that kind of river."[6] For centuries residents along the two-thousand-mile river had tried to tame its flow with a series of walls and levees, but oftentimes to no avail. The river had overflowed its banks dozens of times since the eighteenth century with horrible and, many times, supernatural effects, some including the complete redirection of the river itself. More than one stop along the snaking Mississippi showed signs of the river's presence at one point in history, only to have moved many miles east or west. Towns like Vicksburg that had enjoyed status in one generation as a port city might, in the next generation, be forced to build a canal system just to reach the redirected path of the river.

In the spring of 1927, the rainfall had been much more than usual, and word of levee breaks began to reach every town along the river. By April, the river crested so high above flood stage that waters threatened every community within thirty to fifty miles either east or west. In every town, large or small, men and women worked side by side placing sandbags to reinforce dams, levees, and various makeshift structures, attempting to push back the rushing wall of water.

Elizabeth and Maxine's community was no different. But the waters had risen before, and the river had tested the levees. The levee in their particular community had held for decades and, unlike many along the river, was thought to be well taken care of by the town's fathers. Yet as word came of impending troubles, Thomas prepared to send Elizabeth and their children to Jackson, Mississippi, to stay with relatives. After all, their home sat only a few hundred yards from the river. Even if the levees were to hold, the town would surely see an influx of refugees from other communities not so lucky. As was customary, Maxine would go with Elizabeth, along with Maxine's children. Robert would stay and help Thomas and the others reinforce the town's levee. Elizabeth and Maxine made their way to Jackson, prepared for several days awaiting word that everything was okay. Unfortunately, that word never came.

The levee in Elizabeth's town was not nearly as strong and reliable as first thought. As Thomas, Robert, and the others began inspecting the massive structure, they discovered a series of small breaches that, as the waters grew, jeopardized the integrity of the entire levee. Thus late in the April evening, men, numbering in the hundreds, filled sandbags in a frantic effort to fortify the levee wall.

As was reported later by a witness who watched events unfold from the top of a church in town, the first sign of real trouble came with a rumbling sound similar to that of a locomotive. The water had begun to wash over the top of the levee when, one by one, small internal sections near-er the levee's base began to leak. Within moments the small leaks grew in dramatic fashion, and within an instant a giant section of the levee disintegrated in a huge, violent rush of water. The witness noted that what looked like three or four dozen men standing at the base of the levee in one moment plodding away at their sandbags were in the next moment simply gone.

The bodies of Robert and Thomas were found only a dozen feet or so from each other, but nearly two miles from the levee break. Elizabeth and Thomas's home, along with most other homes and structures in town, was nearly destroyed. The levee break ran some thirty miles inward with massive damage left in its wake. Thousands of people became displaced refugees in a matter of minutes, and whole histories were wiped away.

The Great Flood of 1927 changed the course of the Mississippi Delta. Seven hundred thousand people were displaced and nearly twenty-seven thousand square miles were flooded.[7] Even months after the primary breaks, flood waters remained for miles with some low-lying areas transformed into lake communities forever. The culture and people also changed. Many African Americans migrated north following the flood, searching for a better life but also escaping the intensity of poor treatment by white landowners during the flood's aftermath. Whole communities, economies, and cultures turned in upon themselves, and a rash of racial and social unrest, sitting just below the surface prior to the flood, found its way to the top in violent and unjust ways. For many, the Great Flood served as a recalibration for seeing and experiencing the plight of classes so often forgotten and marginalized.

The worlds of Elizabeth and Maxine would never be the same. They would not return to the Delta for several weeks, remaining many miles away as they grieved together the loss of their husbands and lives. When they did return and the flood waters had receded, it was to a very different life. Their families lived together in the same house, at another large plantation home miles from the river, also owned by Elizabeth's family. But during those days together, their relationship changed in deeper, more profound ways. Their conversations found substance as they talked of memories and feelings about their husbands and earlier years. They realized a common spirit from their childhoods and spent countless hours talking as equals and friends. Elizabeth even convinced Maxine to stop calling her "Ms. Elizabeth" and to stop wearing her maid's uniform, except in public where the uniform made life easier for Maxine. When they were together, no one mistook their relationship as employer and servant; instead, they were two women who shared common stories and common losses.

The flood also gave rise to a refurbished Ku Klux Klan and a power structure that promoted increased segregation and division. Thus, Elizabeth and Maxine's newfound friendship was seen as uncomfortable and inappropriate. It was under this guise, nearly three years after the Great Flood, that a contingent of other prominent leaders in town confronted Elizabeth about her family's closeness with Maxine, feeling that such a prominent white family should not mix so closely with an African American maid. The leaders sat in the parlor of Elizabeth's home, politely dismantling the nature of their friendship, appealing to tradition and heritage as precursors. Finally after hearing the various arguments (not to mention veiled threats), Elizabeth set down her teacup, stood, and said, "Friends, you have come here as supposedly good Christians. You enter my home with intentions of reminding me no less of my family's standing and of the importance that we have held in this community for generations. You speak to me as friends, using the appropriate words and courtesies." Elizabeth paused and gently clasped her hands together.

"But you have mistaken my relationship with Maxine and her family as simply another relationship bound by the same bonds that we have known for decades.... You have missed an important part." Elizabeth looked carefully at each of her visitors before beginning again.

"What you have missed is that my relationship with Maxine runs deeper than friendship. My connection to her is not as maid or employer. I do not see our relationship being determined by social status or a lack thereof.... No ... what I see is a woman who, like me, lost the love of her life. Who must face the next years grieving that loss and trying to make sense for herself, as well as for her children, out of this tragic thing that has happened."

Elizabeth could feel her anger rising, and as much as she wanted to scold her guests for their ignorance, she also did not want to wade into their trap of words and outdated ideas. She paused, looked down, and then said softly, "Gentlemen, we have for generations lived at the bend of this river. We have seen our fortunes made here and lives enriched by its trade. All of us know the power of this river." The crowd seemed quiet, not just in tones but in spirit, for each of them knew of the river's importance in providing for their lives and, in some instances, nearly taking them.

Elizabeth continued, "Maxine and I grew up watching this river, I from my mansion and she from the porch of a sharecropper's shack. We played by this river as children. Both of us were married within yards of it, and both of us would walk with our husbands in quiet, stolen moments, gazing at the setting sun over the river's western bank. It was by the bend in this river that we saw the best of our lives formed, and it is by the bend of this river that our lives changed forever.

"Gentlemen, we all look around and separate ourselves one from another, Negro, white, rich, poor, first-generation Delta family or Northern transplant—we have learned separation as a way of surviving. And yet in an instant, the bend in the river equalizes us, and we learn how to see our neighbors as clearly as we see ourselves."

The room was incredibly silent, an eerie reminder that when truth meets a culture's darker side, our normal responses seem flawed and insignificant. But Elizabeth was not trying to win a debate or prevail in an argument. These words were real and personal, even part confession. She had lived her entire life believing that human relations fit neatly within a particular order. The river had shown her differently. Elizabeth guessed she had always known, though, known what Maxine had always been feeling, known that there really wasn't much difference between the two of them except for money and possessions.

The meeting ended in the quiet, but Elizabeth knew it was not over. Things would change even more now; the signs were already evident. But she also knew that she had changed too. Over the next years, the fortunes of her family and her town suffered. The flood had altered not only the landscape but the economy as well. Elizabeth was forced to adjust her lifestyle, but it was a sacrifice she didn't seem to mind. Eventually, the old plantation home was restored, but not to its original state. There never seemed to be enough resources or will, for that matter. Maxine and she watched as their children grew up and moved. The Delta community did not possess the same possibilities as before, and the younger generation drifted away.

Elizabeth and Maxine found themselves alone, occupying the large home, traipsing about in an echo of part bygone glory and part slavery. Their daily routine rarely changed. They attended to any business needs in the morning and to other various chores and errands in the afternoon. By late afternoon, they returned home to prepare an early supper, but before they dined, they enjoyed a cup of tea on the front porch where they watched the river bend.

One afternoon, Elizabeth remarked, "Isn't it amazing, Maxine, how much of the same world two people can watch without ever knowing the other cares about it too?" Maxine looked over and smiled. "Two different homes, two different views, but always the same river."

Maxine said, "I guess that's what gets folks in trouble.... Only seeing the current from one point of view." With that, Elizabeth gently touched Maxine's hand and watched the water flow.

Flowing Like a River

Take away from me the noise of your songs;
I will not listen to the melody of your harps.
But let justice roll down like waters,
and righteousness like an ever-flowing stream.
(Amos 5:23-24)

This passage of scripture is painful to read. Clearly, God has grown tired of disregard by God's people. The words speak openly of God's justice and of God's inability to exist in the presence of disobedience. If one were to stop at these words in their understanding of God, the picture is frightening and hopeless. The justice of God gives us a glimpse into the intensity of God's character. Left to the description of Amos and barring a miracle of cosmic proportions, our prospects for drawing close to God are impossible, for like a rushing wall of water, the flow of justice and righteousness is unstoppable.

But push the scene forward several hundred years to a place called

Bethlehem, and we find our miracle. The grace of God's heart, a grace that seems to stand flatly against God's justice. An event in Bethlehem provides hope in the form of a child named Jesus. Whereas the lack of justice would seem to disconnect God from God's people in the most tangible and fierce ways, the mercy of God enlists God's own life in our restoration. And thus, along with a carpenter from Nazareth and an unsuspecting virgin girl, God practices and offers authentic *mercy* living, exemplifying for all of us that God's mercy informs God's justice and our capacity to "let justice roll down like waters."

Authentic *mercy* living shared openly in the way described by Jesus potentially changes the way most of us see the world. This is not simply a "good vibe" blessing whereby listeners feel compelled and encouraged to do nice things. On the contrary, it is a call to wholeness and freedom— the freedom to experience our world in a most real and meaningful way. What would happen if people took the time to put themselves in the shoes of others? How would that affect the way we respond, think, and feel about others and their situations? Would it change the way we think of social issues? Would it alter our own expectations for what is just and right? Most important, would it fundamentally transform our hopes, fears, prejudices, and standards? I believe it would.

Authentic *mercy* living is an active compassion and response to the world. It provides for both kindness and accountability. To be in another's experience allows us to hold each other accountable but with a sense of restoration, not condemnation. John 3:17 states, "God did not send the Son into the world to condemn the world, but in order that the world might be saved through him." If God, who has every right to condemn, chooses not to do so, then shouldn't we also practice incarnation compassion with each other?

Authentic *mercy* living, since we are seeing the world not from our own perspective but from the perspective of another, raises tolerance, forgiveness, and servanthood to new levels. Jesus presents authentic *mercy* living as an opportunity to bridge the gaps of broken relationships, between God and humanity, and among human beings as well. One pastor friend describes the fifth blessing as God's means for *slowing down our prejudices, fears, and intolerances, so we might have a chance to see the world as God has chosen to see it.* God forgoes the formalities of creation and becomes a cosmic, spiritual neighbor, setting up house in the midst of our lives. This does not negate the sovereignty of God, but provides a humble sense of knowing that a king has moved into your *community* for the sole purpose of seeing and living like you. God, through Jesus, practiced authentic *mercy* living by deciding to do life with us. And this imprint is all over us.

Nowhere is this seen more clearly than in the lives of children. Jesus said, "Let the little children come *to* me, and do not stop them; for it is *to such as these* that the kingdom of heaven belongs" (Matthew 19:14, emphasis added). As my wise great-aunt used to say, Jesus does not speak just to hear himself talk. There is something to this scripture that we need to see, a glimpse into what authentic *mercy* living is supposed to look like. Children do not worry about perception the way adults do. They see life in simpler, more vivid colors, always watching for the next opportunity to fend off pirates, save the day, and join another exciting adventure. Childhood friendships often show the essence of authentic community, of living life from another's perspective. Sure, there are always fighting and fussing, but there is little actual duplicity with children. Fussing and fighting are about important things, like who made it to first base, the runner or the tag. Whenever children do exhibit maliciousness, as sometimes seen in the news, it looks very much like what adults have been doing to each other for years. Such reports remind us that the bleed-over from adult maladies infects our children.

A pediatrician friend believes part of the problem is too much television and video games and not enough sidewalks and front porches. In my childhood neighborhood, it was a race to see who could get outside first. Television involved three channels (I do remember getting cable in the sixth grade), and video games took up rooms and, as technology progressed, whole tables. You certainly couldn't fit them into your book bag. People sat on their front porches, not secluded decks with privacy fences, and no one had a garage door that opened and closed at will. Families lived in the same houses for years, not months, and everyone knew who lived next door. Seclusion was reserved for those *strange* folks who obviously didn't know the rule: *neighborhood means being neighbors.*

"You can't show real mercy unless you take time to know one another" is my paraphrase of Jesus' fifth blessing. "Don't know how it works?"

God asks. "Well, then watch and I will show you." The next things humanity sees are angels singing and shepherds and wise men following stars. Funny how the salvation of the world began not with God *doing* anything but with God *becoming* like us. The world was not the same again. No glorified tissue dispensing for God; this work required personal time and effort. God acted not because God was bored and decided to display some celestial magic, but because the God of the universe decided that we human beings were actually worth something—in fact, everything. "His mercy flows in wave after wave on those who are in awe before him" (Luke 1:50 *Message*). Now that is a river worth watching!

Notes

1. http://www.brainyquote.com/quotes/quotes/m/mothertere114250.html.

2. Ibid.

3. William Barclay, *The Gospel of Matthew*, vol. 1 (Louisville: Westminster John Knox Press, 2001), 118-19.

4. Ibid., 120.

5. The story is loosely based on an account told to me by a friend who lives in the Mississippi Delta. I created the characters and peripheral details to fill out the story. My source data about the flood is from the official Web site of the event. http://www.pbs.org/wgbh/amex/flood/maps/.

6. Ibid.

7. Ibid.

The Sixth Blessing
Seeing Only What
We Are *Able* to See

Blessed are the pure in heart, for they will see God.
—*Matthew 5:8*

The best and most beautiful things in the world cannot be seen nor even touched, but just felt within the heart.
—*Helen Keller*[1]

A Beary Serious Promise

My children love stuffed animals. As we have traveled across the country, it never fails that we return with a new set of furry creatures donning any number of new accessories. The trend today goes far beyond simply picking out a new stuffed friend at a local toy or department store. The adoption of a stuffed animal is a personal, almost spiritual experience for the children. For me, acquiring these animals is a serious invasion of my wallet and makes me feel like a pack mule; however, I try to handle my bitterness with grace. I realize that I have no choice. Neither does any other doting father.

My children's favorite stuffed animal "adoption agency" (store) provides every sort of creature imaginable. As you walk in, their furry, lifeless exteriors, skins to be stuffed after purchase, line a wall, ready for some loving child to take them home. My children have adopted two dogs, a snake, an odd-looking dinosaur that actually looks like another dog, a monkey we named Clois, and an assortment of bears ranging in themes from your traditional teddy bears to baseball bear, St. Patrick's Day bear, princess bear, and lest we forget, blue devil bear (my favorite).

After the furry skin is selected, each child then goes to a large stuffing machine that reminds me of a local street popcorn vendor. Here the children pump the cotton stuffing into the limbs, giving form and shape to their new friends. For a person with birdlike legs, I have often envied the process, although the whole scene of inserting a metal tube while being spun around to make sure the stuffing is evenly distributed does not appear comfortable. Then, we move to the "heart" section of the assembly line. This part includes the selection of a small red heart placed lovingly into the bear. Before they do so, however, the adopting children must hold the little red heart close to them and promise to love the stuffed animal with all of *their* hearts. As bizarre as the last scene seems, it is touching.

Finally, the bear goes through a series of other labors such as "fluffing" or a "bear beauty shop" as my six-year-old calls it, the addition of sounds (we have always discouraged stopping at this particular section), and the naming of the new family member complete with birth certificate and other "official papers." It is a very thorough process and feels to me as though it takes as long as actual childbirth without, of course, being called ugly names by my wife. And as I get my sales receipt, I believe it costs as much too.

But with all of my complaining, there is something magical about the process, especially when I look at the faces of my daughters and see the joy and love they have for their new friends. Call me a sucker or pushover, but it is such sweet foolishness!

But, before we leave the store, the girls must commit to one final promise. It is the new "Bear Mom Promise" and goes something like this:

I chose this new friend and helped bring her to life.
I promise to always love, cherish, and care for my new friend.
My new friend is special to me and I will always treat her as such.

Every time I watch this, my heart fills with a sense of thankfulness (not to mention my eyes with tears) as I see my beautiful girls make the deepest of commitments. Their faces are serious; their eyes focused; their hearts genuine. I realize that what they are doing is real and pure for them. And each time I hear them make that promise, I think of the days they were born and similar words I uttered to God.

Contaminated Versus Compromised

Through the sixth blessing, Jesus suggests that our "pure in heart" moments most define the other moments of our lives. The Greek word translated *pure* in Matthew 5:8 is *katharos,* which is defined both as a state of being and as an ongoing process of purification, with the "purifier" constantly aware and active in "weeding out" impure influences around him or her. *Katharos* suggests an ongoing awareness of remaining pure with equal opportunities for success or failure. And to take the meaning of the word further, every thought or action related to *katharos* or the process of being made pure signifies an effect on its surroundings. Thus, *katharos* is not only important for the "purified" in question; it is also important because the process has a real impact on others. As a truck driver friend stated after listening to my explanation of pure, "It don't matter how pretty the clothes. If you ain't bathed in a month, you still gonna stink!" Beautifully put![2]

Jesus understood that real purity is more about what is driving the desire for purity—our motives resting deep within us—than the simple product or outward manifestation of a clean, rules-abiding life. In Jesus' day, the Pharisees had mastered the act of pure living better than anyone. They had religion down to an art and could pray, speak, and even walk as if they were completely in step with God. However, time and again, Jesus warned the Pharisees about outward appearances, insisting that it was the heart that dictated real purity. *It truly matters more* why *you are doing than simply the act of doing* was Jesus' consistent refrain. This required a life of real self-examination that reflected deeply on the internal motives of a person's life, not just whether all of the actions looked good.[3]

A friend of mine says that a person is what he or she really is, no more, no less. For years, I wondered if my friend's exciting, but taxing college days had left some cognitive disruption, especially with a saying like this, until I took the time to understand what she meant. People are who they are deep down, no matter what they say or do. Kinda like *you are what you eat*—but for the soul. The King James Version of Proverbs 23:7 reads, "For as he thinketh in his heart, so is he." The proverb is an admonition against eating the bread of the stingy who tell you to eat and drink. If you do, you will vomit (Proverbs 23:8 KJV). The New Revised Standard Version of Proverbs 23:7 states, "For like a hair in the throat, so are they." Jesus echoes this tradition of humor when he challenges those among the scribes and Pharisees who "clean the outside of the cup and of the plate" but are on the inside "full of greed and self-indulgence" (Matthew 23:25 NRSV). He continues, "First clean the inside of the cup, so that the outside also may become clean" (Matthew 23:26 NRSV). I have concluded that this is not about every thought or image that runs through my head (thank goodness!) but about the genesis of these thoughts. What causes people to say something? But even more important, what do they really mean to say? When Jesus says that the pure in heart will see God, he is talking about those whose deepest parts and motives are clean and pure.

To understand this level of purity in our lives requires incredible self-examination, and to be quite honest, most human beings are resistant because it can be very painful and shameful. But Jesus insists that unless we are first willing to look deep within ourselves and discover *why* we are who are, we will not be able to experience the fullness of God around us.

The Flying Tomato

Shaun White is a skinny, red-headed professional snowboarder and skateboarder from Carlsbad, California, who might very well be the coolest kid in America or, at least, my children think so. Not only has Shaun won every major title in snowboarding, but he has set most of the world records with a distinctive panache that is oddly humble. He simply snowboards, rumbling through the pikes with such flare and ease as to make any of us think that we can do it. Shaun White is a prodigy of snowboarding. As you watch him, you realize that for Shaun it is not about the fame or the fortune. He snowboards because he loves it!

Nowhere was this more evident than at the 2006 Winter Olympics in Turin, Italy. Clearly the favorite prior to the games, Shaun approached the event with the same laid back, dedicated fervor that had carried him through the Grand Prix series victories a month earlier. To most Olympic observers, it wasn't *if* Shaun would win, but *how bad* would he win. Thus, everyone was shocked after the first day to find Shaun not only out of the top spot, but in danger of not making the finals at all. A rare fall during the first round left Shaun needing a second round rout to make it into the second series of runs.

As he approached the start, all eyes were on Shaun, wondering if his would be a fate similar to other well-appointed athletes who simply could not perform when the time came. However, much to the relief of all Tomato fans, as well as innumerable sponsors, Shaun proceeded to qualify for the second round and to take the lead with what remains one of the best snowboarding exhibitions ever. Shaun's daring maneuvers transfixed the watching audience and the judges. He would go on to win the gold by a landslide.

Following the event, I remember one of the commentators, in an offhanded remark, stated that Shaun White didn't just win; he captured the victory. The commentators talked about how the best snowboarders don't just win championships; they perform as though they have consciously removed defeat as an option. Having been in love with sports my whole life, I realized this was more than being "in the zone." This is an entirely different level of competition and execution.

It hit me that Shaun White won as much for the way he approached the event as for how he executed it. When things seemed so bleak, needing an unbelievable run just to make the second round, most athletes would have allowed the pressure of the moment to focus them on what could go wrong. Shaun White and those like him see so purely the nature of what they do that they can see only victory. Defeat is unimaginable, a non-negotiable, in their scheme of processing. It was apparent to me that Shaun White made the run look so easy because he was just doing what he loved. To most people, Olympic glory would be hanging in the balance, but to Shaun White, a pure lover of his sport, it was another run.

After the interview, my family sat with several friends and watched as the "Flying Tomato," as he was called on TV, smiled through one autograph after another. One friend stated, "See how happy he looks." Another friend replied, "Wouldn't you be if you had just won a gold medal?" The first friend responded, "I've seen that smile before. He's not smiling about the gold medal; he's smiling because he nailed the run!" I can still see an indelible image of Shaun White holding his hands high in the air because he had won and also because he had seen in himself exactly what he was created to be.

Raised Hands

The pure in heart understand the driving desire of their lives and live each day as a perpetual response. In a world with so many false emotions, motives, and schemes, we are afforded glimpses of genuine faith and life, sometimes in the most unexpected places. But, Jesus' sixth blessing suggested that even in a glimpse we would see nothing short of God.

I saw this one Valentine's Day when my wife and I took our two oldest daughters to the concert of a popular Christian artist. During the closing moments of the concert, the mood changed dramatically into what could only be explained as a massive worship experience. With the words projected on the screen behind the stage, nearly seven thousand concert goers began singing and praising God. I, too, was moved by the experience, and, although I am not prone to public displays of emotion, I found myself, eyes closed and face toward heaven, raising my hands in praise. I was completely lost in the moment until my wife gently touched my shoulder. I opened my eyes to see her motioning subtly to our left. I saw our nine-year-old daughter with her hands, palms up, raised. Her eyes were closed, and her face had a sweet expression, more beautiful than anything I have ever seen. For a moment, I stood and watched my daughter praise God and realized that in that little heart was a pure, sincere connection to the Creator of this universe. I also knew that I wasn't just watching my daughter, but I was privy to a holy moment between God and one of God's dear children. It was nothing short of awesome.

On the ride home, I asked my daughters about the concert. They both loved the music, lights, and noise, but my middle daughter (age six at the time) interjected, "I didn't like people raising their hands." Before I could respond, my oldest daughter replied, "Well, that's how some people praise God, Juli Anna."

Juli Anna quickly retorted, "Raising my hands would embarrass me." It struck me that this comment came from the same girl who did a cartwheel in front of hundreds of people on the lawn outside the entrance to the coliseum. All of us have our own ways of getting God's and others' attentions.

My oldest daughter thought a minute and then said, "Well, I had to raise my hands."

Finding this curious, I asked why. "Because, Daddy," she said, "in my heart I wanted to raise them, but was afraid to. Then I heard God's voice say, 'Don't be afraid to let people know you love me.'" I looked back, and my daughter had the most sincere look on her face as she continued, "And then I just raised them, and..." She stopped a moment.

"Honey," I said. "What is it?" My daughter caught my eye in the rear-view mirror and, with a look that could only be described as heavenly, said, "It was just beautiful, just beautiful." Yes, the pure in heart really can see God.

Seeing Only What We Are *Able* to See

As a prejudiced, doting father, I am privileged with intimate views of my children's lives. Often, I can't see my own life clearly. I am too jaded, too closed off from my faults. Most of us want to see the best in our children or to hope the best for them. We all want to view them in the most flattering light. But, certainly, children also offer moments that are not so good. The terrible twos are just the first period in their lives when our children express their independence by letting us know that things do not suit them. Parenting is not always fun! Yet I believe children offer the closest and best examples of a simple and pure view of life. They remind us that not too terribly long ago, we, too, viewed the world with the simplicity and sweetness of children. And, I am glad that our jaded lives never quite disconnect from the hope of our childhoods.

Jesus knew this purity in children. He knew that in each child there is a purity of such magnitude that it becomes the doorway for seeing God. He said, "Let the little children come to me, and do not stop them; for it is to such as these that the kingdom of heaven belongs" (Matthew 19:14). Jesus' words were more than just a plea for children, but a call to all of us that we might remember our own doorways of purity and hope as glimpses of God. However, the responsibilities of this world and the drivenness of adulthood often prevent us from seeing the real work of God around us. Our motives and desires often cloud our perceptions of good, faithful living and cause us to miss the very meaning that we seek in our lives. Our relationships become symbols of status or position instead of genuine interactions for building community. Our work develops our bank accounts instead of gifts and graces for the good of others. Our service cements our résumés instead of pricking our hearts and lives to live generously. Our congregational life centers on obligation and expectation instead of moments in the presence of God. All the while we convince ourselves that we have lived faithfully, worked diligently, and shared openly, but we have missed the real meaning—accomplishing all of this *with* God, not just *for* God.

Jesus knew that living in such a pattern, we lose sight of God in our midst. We become too occupied with *producing* for God's kingdom. The only alternative is a turning in of our faith until it becomes more ritualistic and self-serving. And after some time, we become like a person lost in a cave, whose vision eventually deteriorates from the lack of light and focus. After a while, we could fill the cave with light, but the person's eyes could not stand it.

And yet another result is that we become "dumb" to our surroundings in such profound ways as to skew our impression of reality. One of my favorite movies is *Cast Away*, in which Tom Hanks's character is stranded on a deserted island with only a few FedEx packages to keep him company. In one of the packages is a volleyball, which at first appears useless for a man trapped on an island. But over time, Hanks's character, so starved for companionship, turns the volleyball into a working partner and friend, even to the point of painting a face on the ball. The volleyball became the trusted friend, Wilson, because of a stranded man's inability to see any other relationship. He would rather turn to the absurd than be alone.

One of the saddest scenes in the movie occurs when Hanks's character must choose between a life raft and Wilson. As absurd as it appears, the scene is stark and emotional, for we all have suffered the pain of loss, even when that which is lost provides little real connection or value. In the end, Jesus states (and I paraphrase the beatitude) a *clouded heart cannot see God.* Nor can a clouded heart imagine real connection to God and neighbor.

A Nice Lady

Just a few weeks ago, my second and third grade Sunday school teacher died after a long and debilitating illness. Ms. Gandy was a small, petite lady who possessed a quiet nature and sweet spirit. She wore thick glasses, at least all of my life, and spoke with a gentle tone that required you to listen carefully just to hear what she was saying.

I remember Ms. Gandy for the way she greeted you when you walked into her class. She would smile, open her arms, and beckon you to come give her a hug. Ms. Gandy believed kids learned best while they were having fun; therefore, our Sunday school class was less Bible instruction and more guided play with a Bible theme. Either way you look at it, I probably formed more of my spiritual walk in those two years than at any other time in my life.

It was an especially important time for me because my parents had divorced six months prior to my arrival in Ms. Gandy's class. My mother and I moved to our new hometown, and the change generated all of the daunting adjustments of any move including new friends, a new school, and eventually, a new family member in the person of my stepfather. Meeting Ms. Gandy in the midst of this was a breath of fresh air, and I will never forget how she provided, at least for that one day a week, a sense of peace and normalcy for me. She encouraged me to ask questions and to explore the richness of God, whose character I held suspect because of my parents' divorce. Looking back, I think that Ms. Gandy probably did more to save God's reputation in my eyes than anything else. Who says God doesn't need good public relations?

Ms. Gandy also made promises to me as well as to each child she taught. She promised every Sunday to pray for us, and even long after we had moved out of her class, she would stop us and remind us that those prayers were still being lifted to heaven. I am not sure I truly appreciated that sentiment until a couple of years ago during the book signing of my first book. As I sat at the author's table greeting buyers and signing books, I noticed to my left a lady in a wheelchair making her way closer. Stopping to notice her, I realized that it was Ms. Gandy being pushed by her daughter. I got up from my seat and went over to give her a hug. It had been many years since I had seen her. She had suffered from a series of health complications that had left her weak. She had difficulty communicating, but her gentle, sweet spirit was still evident. Ms. Gandy's daughter mentioned that Ms. Gandy was not well, but had insisted, after seeing information of the event in the local newspaper, on coming to the signing. I spent a few moments talking with Ms. Gandy before returning to my seat, but only after she told me, once again, that she was praying for me.

As I told a friend about Ms. Gandy's death, my friend's daughter asked, "Was she a nice lady?"

"Yes, very much," was my reply.

"What made her special?" my little friend responded.

"Her heart," I said.

Ms. Gandy's life was certainly not filled with great accolades or grand accomplishments according to the world's standards, but her grace trumped any achievement and her impact on countless people's lives is unquestioned. No one who remembers her as his or her teacher can forget the sense of seeing Christ in her. You saw this in Ms. Gandy because she could see Christ with such clarity, and this clarity came not from degrees or titles, but from a heart that saw and spoke truthfully to the God of Creation. Her life reflected the light of Christ because her soul was void of the clutter that so often inhibits God's reflection. In Ms. Gandy, it was a beautiful thing to behold.

And Nice Neighbors

Our community is a mixture of middle-class blue-collar people and transplants of all shapes and sizes looking for good schools and safe streets. My particular neighborhood consists of single-family homes, complete with two-car garages and kids playing in the front yard. Although we are by no means a wealthy community, most have more than we need in terms of both resources and potential.

We live at the end of a cul-de-sac, a word I am convinced means "dead end" in French, with a vacant lot on one side and a family of four on the other. My family owns the vacant lot, bought, many say, as a way of controlling access to our small piece of dead-end heaven. They would not be wrong.

Our neighbors are the best anyone could ask for. They are kind, helpful, and incredibly considerate. The family members exude faithfulness to one another, to their friends, and to their church that is unique and enviable in our world. Chris, the father, is a soft-spoken, former business professional who gave up his career of nearly fifteen years to join the staff of his local church as director of recreation and administration. I have never met anyone with more of a gift for details. He is no less than an administrator extraordinaire with a penchant for multi-tasking various levels of jobs and duties.

But Chris's work and life are far from sterile or boring. One cannot talk long with him without gaining a true sense of his commitment to Christ and his genuine love for God's people. The program and administration of the church are Chris's ministry, and he sees every detail from the signs on the doors to the condition of the restrooms as a personal testament to his and his church's love for God.

However, even before joining the church staff, Chris began a recreation ministry that uses basketball to minister to children and their families. Basketball has long been a special part of Chris's life. He has played the game since he was a youngster. In fact, it was from a basketball court nearly twenty years ago, that Chris gave his life to Christ. As he mentions in his own testimony, he believed that his connection to the game ended when he walked off that court, committing his life to wherever God would lead. To think that one day Chris could use basketball as a means for sharing the love of God with others is both irony and treasure.

In the past four years, nearly one thousand kids have been involved in Chris's basketball ministry. In a town whose population is only ten thousand total, this is a remarkable feat. But not if you know Chris. Although administration is his primary and most noticeable gift, it is not the only one with which he has been blessed. Chris also has the gift of evangelism and encouragement. His testimony, spoken in a soft, slow drawl, speaks of God's love in such personal terms that even an experienced preacher and teacher like me is profoundly moved. In fact, people have heard me talk of Chris's testimony so often that they want to know the secret to his success. My response is simple: "When he talks, you believe that what he is saying is true."

For some, this answer does not suffice. Many believe there must be a trick or, at least, some other gimmick that Chris uses to make such an impression, but the opposite is true. He does not attempt to be overly dynamic. He often looks down, glancing up only out of a sense of responsibility. And he shuffles, often from side to side. But Chris is also humble and sincere, and every listener knows that what he is saying comes from the deepest parts of his heart. When he finishes speaking, you are more than aware of his message and even more aware of God's love.

Why does Chris's testimony strike such a chord in people? Because when you experience his testimony, you sense God through him. You have such a sense of God because, like Ms. Gandy, Chris's heart sees honestly the presence of God. And once again, like Ms. Gandy, it is a beautiful thing to behold.

Believing Is Seeing

Put two people at a street corner just minutes before an accident and ask them to describe the details, and you will be surprised by the contrasting descriptions. Add a little twist to the story by having one onlooker actually know someone involved in the accident, and the plot thickens. Let's say one of the onlookers is the insurance agent of one of the drivers, and perceptions become even more convoluted. Have one of the bystanders actually own one of the vehicles, and no matter the circumstances, the truth will be in trouble. In this case, *seeing has nothing to do with believing* what actually happened.

Take a blank canvas along with paints and brushes, and put them in the center of a room. Instruct an untrained person to begin to paint, and the outcome will resemble the basic, simple nature of her skill (or lack thereof). Now, take a trained artist and set him at the same blank canvas, and an image will form that is both bearable and meaningful. Then take a master artist, such as Rothko, Matisse, or Picasso, and place him at this blank canvas, and you will see the creation of a masterpiece. For the untrained artist, the motive is to put paint on a canvas. For the trained artist, the motive is to form an image. But for the master artist, the motive is to create magic. An artist's clarity determines her ability in helping us believe in what she creates.

The same is true for our spiritual lives. Of all the blessings, the sixth one most reminds me of my grandmother. Her life spoke to the importance of purity and hope in a person's life in helping her see the heart of God. Although she experienced numerous difficulties and trials, she never, beyond all explanation, lost sight of God's presence. For her, every day was an opportunity to draw closer to God and to see the mystery of God's love and grace unfold. As with a master artist, her clarity of heart, uncluttered by the desires and motives of this world, determined how well she could see God, and how well she could see God determined how well others could see God through her.

Jesus understood that purity of heart gives people an advantage that the world can not. It gives stability and a fresh footing when things begin to shift. It allows for reflection and learning from our troubles instead of spiritual paralysis; and it fosters a sense of true humility and hope that God is present and working for our good. "Draw near to God, and [God] will draw near to you" (James 4:8). This scripture always puzzled me until read against the backdrop of this blessing. God has already drawn close to us, but like any one searching and groping in this world, we must learn to take hold of what is right in front of us—to grasp even what we cannot see with our physical eyes. In this realm, it is *believing that is seeing*, and we can only believe fully as we have fully removed all of those obstacles that blind our view. And, thus, read, seen, and lived against this truth, purity of heart matters.

Notes

1. http://www.afb.org/braillebug/hkfacts.asp.
2. William Barclay, *The Gospel of Matthew*, vol. 1 (Louisville: Westminster John Knox Press, 2001), 122-23.
3. *Interpreter's Commentary*, 285.

The Seventh Blessing
Producing *Right* Relationships

Blessed are the peacemakers, for they will be called children of God.
—Matthew 5:9

In the church, we are dared to believe that it is God who makes us a community and not we ourselves, and that our differences are God's best tools for opening us up to the truth that is bigger than we are.
—Barbara Brown Taylor[1]

Flipped

Carol did not necessarily need for me to say hello, and she received my greeting with hesitation. It didn't take much for me to turn around and ask how her day was going, but at the moment it felt like a great effort. I guess in a world that moves with such speed and anonymity, acts of kindness often feel more out of place than they should. Carol, a checker at a large retail grocery store, was busy moving customers through a cattle procession of frozen foods and bagged fruit. She did not stand out; in fact, Carol was very plain and looked like a person who lived a modest life. She was polite, and even though I was not in a particularly good mood, she chatted quietly about the weather. I answered with a few obligatory responses like "yes" and "you're exactly right," my standard, people-passing conversation responses, until the checkout was complete and the receipt was in my hand. Carol said, "Have a nice day, sir." I nodded, took my groceries, and proceeded toward the door.

However, not five steps from the checkout aisle, I stopped, plagued by the eeriest feeling that I had forgotten something. I checked in my bags to make sure that everything I purchased was on the list, for I am notorious about forgetting the one most important item for which I was sent to the store. Although everything was accounted for, the uneasiness did not go away. What was it? Suddenly, another feeling hit me, the feeling that I have when I have been looking for my car keys for half an hour only to realize that they have been in my hand all along. I realized what I had missed.

Turning and taking a few steps back to the checkout counter, I approached Carol, who thankfully did not have any customers, and I said, "Carol, please excuse my rude demeanor just a moment ago." Carol seemed surprised and not just a little concerned. I continued, "You were steadily talking to me, and all I could do was grunt a few words. I just wanted to come back and say 'thank you' for what you do but, more than anything, for who you are, and for trying, even when people don't apparently want it, to brighten as many days as you can."

By this time I am sure Carol was convinced that I was not all right, and she simply said, "You're welcome." Customers were lining up, and our conversation needed to move on. I left the store thinking that it didn't take much effort for me to turn and simply be nice, but how much nicer and more effective my comments would have been if I had made them sooner. I do not know what was going on in Carol's life. I am not sure if her day was good or not or if the life she lived was fulfilled. All I know is that on this day, I stood as a well-educated, well-to-do Christian, feeling very dumb, very poor, and very unChristlike.

Recently, a friend introduced me to a new children's book titled *Flipped*. Written by Wendelin Van Draanen Parsons, the much acclaimed story involves two elementary-aged children experiencing the daily twists and routines of friendship and growing up.[2] The book is unique in that it allows the reader a glimpse into the psyche of both characters by "flipping" the chapters—one read from the perspective of the boy, Bryce, and the other from the girl, Julianna. It is a wonderful story filled with all of the nuances of young boys and girls finding their real hearts and souls, not to mention the confusion and speculation of a first kiss. The readers weave through a magical, yet simple, story, flipping from one character's train of thought to the other, all the while feeling as though they are spinning above them, watching their lives unfold. The writing is creative with a familiar storyline.

The most important lesson I learned from the book was that everyone around us has a perspective of whatever situation might be unfolding. Everyone also has feelings, emotions, sensitivities, hurts, and dreams associated with these perspectives, and it is highly likely that all these are different from ours. *Flipped* reminded me that we are intricately connected to one another, and although it is easy to see life from only our point of view, our connectedness is powerful. Whether we are second graders pondering the boy who moves in next door, eighth graders fearfully and wonderfully expecting a first kiss, or adult checkout clerks working at a grocery store, we all have an important place. Taking the time to see our place beside another's teaches us to prevent or to mend many wounds down the road.

Why God Hears Falling Trees

I believe that if a tree falls in the woods and no one is there to hear it, it *most certainly* makes a sound. I would ask, however, "Does anyone care?" I am not trying to be coy, but apart from the relational nature of someone noticing, measuring, or attributing significance to the tree's fall, does the fact that it makes any or no sound actually have a bearing on the tree's existence, on its potential for growth, or on its death? I would say no. Even in the forest, the relational aspects of existence define and shape reason.

Thankfully, the presence of God, who perceives everything and who is always in relationship with creation, ensures that the tree does exist, is not a figment of humanity's imagination even when not seen, and does, indeed, make a sound. God has wired the world for creation to exist in simultaneous relationship, and we are incredibly interdependent one to another. This was not some cosmic experiment for God. Human beings are created to need one another, and when that formula fails, the very essence of our nature is wounded. Relationships are a spiritual portal by which God experiences creation and by which we experience God. Therefore, when relationships break down, part of our connection to God also suffers.

As Jesus shares the seventh blessing, notice that he does not say that the peace*lovers* will be called children of God. The wording is "blessed are the peace*makers.*" Those who *make* peace, not just want it, will be called sons and daughters. Jesus knows the value of right relationships and understands the fragile bond of how we do life together. Working for peace includes the whole of a person's life. For some, it might be working diligently to bring peace and justice to the social conditions of the world. Truly blessed are those who work to make the world a better place for all people.[3] There are many examples in our world of these kinds of peacemakers. We need look only to Gandhi, Rosa Parks, or Mother Teresa to see the value of giving one's life to peacemaking in righting the ills of humanity. Every day, all over the world, people fight for equality and restoration as a means of serving the immediate needs of people and addressing the long-term causes of division and mistrust. Look at the work of Bono with debt relief in Africa or Jim Wallis with the Sojourners ministry, and you will find peacemakers of great purpose. No one would argue that their efforts at peacemaking serve a deeper, more divine call.

For others, peacemaking may primarily mean working to restore the relationship between humanity and God. Truly blessed are those who work to connect to God. We see the personal and spiritual elements of our lives, whatever they are, as doorways for seeing God.[4] During my ministry, I worked with countless individuals who were at war with God because of past hurts, misunderstandings, personal mistakes, you name it. Their anger kept them from seeing God's work in their lives and from experiencing the real sense of what they craved most, namely, peace. I believe that part of being a peacemaker is to approach the Creator with our baggage of anger, worry, and pain and to lay it at God's feet. Only then can we experience the beauty of a life without such weight and burden.

However, I believe Jesus' primary intention for us is to view peacemaking in terms of all of our relationships, whether with God or each other. To work at building together instead of dividing helps us to see a glimpse of God's life and work in our world. A life committed to relationship building will not go unrewarded or unblessed, even when efforts fail or turn in directions different from those intended. Not all of my relationship building has been successful in its original intentions, but it has been always beneficial. Jesus is talking not about events or moments of building, but about a lifetime pattern.[5] For us to truly see God, we must first work as God does in our midst, carefully replacing and restoring the building blocks of creation, most notably, relationships. When we do this work of peacemaking, then we may be called "children of God."[6]

The Shame of the *Church*

In his article "Confections of Apartheid: A Stick-and-Carrot Pedagogy for the Children of Our Inner City Poor," Jonathan Kozol describes the increasing resegregation of American education in the twenty-first century based, in this latest version, less on race and more on socioeconomic realities.[7] An award-winning author and educator, Kozol has watched American schools for more than forty years, delineating the increasing institutional nature of education and disconnection of children from meaningful, relationship-building structures and opportunities and who are subjected to this institutional model as a means of "ordering" the educational experience to control discipline and to maximize resource allocation. In the process, these models herd children into educational patterns that rely more on regurgitating information than on developing and sustaining learning skills. Even more distressing, in the deemphasizing of holistic learning, community and relationships are also placed in jeopardy.[8]

As Kozol outlines his argument, he discusses several classroom experiences in which he witnessed instructional practice. Time and again, he describes teachers and children bound by rigid educational systems more intent on processing information than helping children to build learning and community enrichment skills. Absolutely no theatrics or "kids being kids," in these environments learning is serious business.[9] Kozol fears that our systems of education are doing better jobs at creating future prisoners than productive, creative citizens. And the disconnection of children from learning how to be in community raises a serious disruption in the development of much needed people skills, all the while placing the children and society as a whole at risk.[10]

The work riveted me because it detailed a systematic disconnection of students from one another and from the ability to build workable, meaningful community.[11] As I finished the article, I was stunned by what the implications of such a system meant for the future of our society. How could people think and live faithfully in community if they had never learned or had the opportunity to deal and work together? I recoiled in horror at the thought of my children dealing with other boys and girls unresourced and unequipped for the world. But like any self-interested parent, I was thankful that the examples in Kozol's work dealt with urban schools far away from my own children's educational experience—or so I thought.

After hearing me talk about the article, a friend of mine, who teaches fourth grade, invited me to visit her class. I remember I went on a Tuesday because I thought Tuesday would be more settled than Monday for the kids. I drove to the entrance of the school, complete with its new sign that read "Welcome to a Place Where Children Experience the Exceptional." *Good start*, I thought. *We all want education to be about exceptional ideas and learning.*

My visit to the front desk was also very impressive. The foyer, as I would later discover about the halls and classrooms, was immaculate, and the receptionist carried a very professional air about her. Awards for Excellence, given as the result of rising test scores, lined the walls along with framed posters of every imaginable leadership and excel slogan. And if this were not enough, I noticed there was fresh coffee available for parents and visitors, but a sign read "Refreshments should only be enjoyed in the foyer. Thank you." The receptionist, after checking on my appointment with the teacher, gave me a visitor badge and escorted me to her classroom.

The first thing I noticed about the school itself was how quiet it was. The few kids whom I passed in the hall did not say a word, and as we made our way to my friend's classroom and walked past a window that viewed the playground, I remember the eeriest sense of silence. Usually, children's playgrounds, no matter how well-insulated from the world around them, give off a certain high-pitched squeal as children play. But this playground, although I convinced myself it was just a great sealant on the windows, provided none of this.

We made a right from the hall where we had been walking. But to my left, I saw the entrance to the cafeteria. Asking my guide to wait a second, I turned around and went back to the door to have a look. The cafeteria was as nice as any I had ever seen, and as quiet. Once again, my stereotypes of school cafeterias involved a lot of noise, but the noise was not here. I turned around, and we continued our march to my friend's classroom. As I arrived, my friend, who was at the head of the class giving instructions, acknowledged me with a wink—no smile, just a wink.

The receptionist informed me that I could sit at the back of the class until the break, at which time the teacher could speak with me.

As I took my seat, I noticed that the classroom was very clean and had an exceptional order about it. The kids sat in the traditional rows, books neatly organized under their desks. The walls had posters and learning tools on them, but seemed almost colorless. It was the model classroom—for an adult seminar.

But, nothing that I saw rivaled what I heard; again, nothing except my friend reading what I thought was instruction at first, but as I listened, I realized my friend was reading the lesson itself. The kids, fourth graders, mind you, sat listening, making no sound at all as their teacher delivered a lesson about Antarctica in a monotone. I couldn't believe my eyes or ears. Not only did this seem almost surreal—the walk to the room, the class setup, the kids—but my friend was certainly not herself. She is one of the most animated people I have ever known, and she went into teaching as a way of expressing her love for life with children. But what I saw in front of me, anyone could do, whether he was gifted for teaching or not.

Finally, when the kids were to begin working quietly on their assignments, my friend made her way to the back. She could tell by the look on my face what I was thinking and motioned for me to join her in a makeshift cubicle on the other side of the class. Whispering, of course, she confronted my look by saying, "Not what you expected?"

"No," I said, almost bewildered.

"Real quiet, isn't it?" she replied.

"What is all of this?" I asked.

"This is a new model of school," she replied. "We are having a silent day—no talking allowed except when approached or asked."

"What?" I asked again, realizing that I wasn't exactly asking the smartest of questions.

"Silent day," my friend said again. "No talking in the classroom, except under exceptional circumstances, or in the cafeteria or even on the playground."

"The playground!" I said louder, before my friend shushed me back to a quieter tone.

"It's crap, Shane, just crap," my friend replied. I couldn't help smiling at her answer. She continued, "We're teaching these kids knowledge but not helping them to learn anything, especially about life. They walk around like Stepford children."

"How did this happen?" I asked.

"This is a poor district," she replied. "Discipline was out of control. Test scores were dropping. So the new superintendent introduced this new model of learning. It looks good on paper, but it can't work in the long run. We're teaching kids to think in boxes, and the boxes don't even belong to them."

"What about the parents? Don't they see this as a problem?" I asked.

"The parents are primarily underresourced and undereducated. They just don't react the way upper-middle-class parents would. The system knows this and takes advantage of it. Shane, we're not building a community of learners. This is a training school for good inmates."

My friend's comments struck me. What I had read in Kozol's book was taking place within a couple of days driving distance from my home. In fact, I learned later that many districts had moved to this form of instruction and school order. And I also learned that my children's schools, although they didn't practice this extreme, did have policies whereby, if forced to choose between community and order, always seemed to side with order. And it hit me as I left my friend's school that it had an eerie peace about it, but only in the way that you define peace as the absence of conflict. It was certainly not teaching the children to be peacemakers; they were learning to conform to the norm, no matter how disconnected it seemed. I looked at the sign on my way out. *Yes*, I thought, *this was truly an exceptional, if not disturbing, experience for me.*

But in truth, it is not exceptional for our society, especially for the church. We have been sitting in rows and asking people to be silent for years, all the while expecting, between the homily and the periodic covered dish, that people might actually learn how to take their faith and make it real. The real purpose is not community, though; it is order. And we have lived with an *order over community* mind-set for generations, choosing discipline over really experiencing the fullness of faith in God. And thus, we have sacrificed our potential for building deep, committed relationships.

Watching this school and thinking about the real needs of human beings, I understood Jesus' seventh blessing. Blessed are those who work to make relationships and then nurture them so they are meaningful and right. We are wired for this, and in its absence, we simply cannot be whole. The nature of community, whether it is over a lunchroom table or across a pew, does more to show us God and God's work than any other thing on earth. So we must ask the question, why do people (most of us anyway) prefer to live in order, even if it means sacrificing real community? The answer, I believe, is as old as ages and has more to do with not being hurt than it does being really real.

The Beat of a Broken Heart

Some people have a gift of saying stupid things, and I am one of these people. A friend of mine is married to one of the sweetest, most attractive people I have ever known. For years, I picked on him about "marrying above himself" and about how he should be thankful to be married to a woman like that. I also used the phrasing, as guys are prone to do, that he better "watch out or someone will try to steal her." My comments were always playful and seemingly meant nothing.

However, one day while we were playing golf, my friend told me that someone had indeed *stolen* his wife from him for a certain period of time. She had an affair that lasted for several years, and she came very close to giving up her family for this person. There were many reasons that their marriage broke down, and he admitted that it was not just her fault. As I listened to him share his heart, I could tell that this was serious business for him. He finished the conversation by saying, "It is the most difficult, unbelievable thing I have ever experienced. I never thought she would break my heart."

I remember standing there in silence, ashamed at all of my gaffs and prior comments, and also deeply moved by my friend's honesty and vulnerability. "I am very sorry; I had no idea," I said.

"We never do," my friend replied.

After a few moments, I asked, "How can you stay with someone who broke your heart like that?"

My friend replied, "Because there is also no one else on earth who makes me happier."

"But can you trust her?" I responded.

"I hope so; I have to believe so," my friend said. "Shane, I may never completely heal from my broken heart, but what I could not survive is not trying." My friend stopped a moment, and I could tell he had walked through this conversation before, possibly with someone else, most certainly in his own heart. He looked up at me again and with a subtle smile said, "Even broken hearts can have a beat, and it is the beat that gives our lives rhythm. I am afraid of when the music stops more than the risk of the dance."

Personally, I don't like broken hearts, although I have not believed in them for very long. For years in my ministry, I would sit and listen to people talk about *their* broken hearts and would wonder if such were truly possible. I understand disappointment, pain, and mourning, but a *broken heart* always seemed so much worse. People described feelings of unbelievable loss and loneliness that, no matter where they were or who they were with, became almost palpable and seemingly unbearable. I chalked up the descriptions to basic depression, learning later that depression is only a part of the dynamic.

The *broken heart* is unique in that nothing on this earth can heal it. Just as our physical hearts are a mixture of complex components providing, in a simple, quite mechanical manner, the very source of life, our emotional hearts are also complicated components of relationships, hopes, desires, and dreams. When our physical hearts are broken, doctors give close attention to what needs to be done for healing. In the most dire cases, a completely new heart may be required for survival. Healing our emotional hearts also requires close attention. We are fashioned from birth with certain vulnerable emotions held deep within us that need the same deep healing when they are injured.

Quite frankly, relationships are the source of both good and bad when it comes to our emotional hearts. Nothing shapes a person's life more than the woven fabrics of relationships, and nothing can hurt as deeply as when these fabrics are torn. Nothing prepares us adequately for working through relationships. Maybe that is why it takes so much effort to guide them and sometimes just to keep them functional. They are fragile and vulnerable, require nurture, and oftentimes seem to require more work than they are worth. And yet it is through relationships that we see the sweetest possibilities and joys of this world—a daughter's laugh, a wife's smile, a friend's care. Relationships are risky business on both an emotional level and a spiritual level.

But many times, it takes great risk to see the greatest rewards in our world. Without the potential of a broken heart, we could not experience the bliss of a heart fulfilled; without the potential of a broken heart, we could not satisfy the longings of a heart in love; and without the potential of a broken heart, we could not exhibit the truest joy of a heart restored. These are not lost words or just the musings of philosophy; they are more theology than anything I have ever known.

God's own heart for us stood at that line of risk. Our relationship with God was born from God's vulnerability in offering freely, through Jesus, a glimpse into the life of God. God was willing to experience rejection for us. No one understands the depth and importance of relationship better than Jesus, because no one better understands the fragile nature and risky behavior of it as well.

When my own heart was broken several years ago, I wondered about God's presence in all of it. If God were truly sovereign, couldn't God have stopped my pain? Couldn't God have waved away, in some magical show, the betrayal and hurt? Sure, God could do that. But God also understands that relationship is the unknown equation of creation. Even when a relationship doesn't work right, it still remains a precious window that shows potential for our souls.

When we are hurt by broken relationships, our tendency is to withdraw, to circle the wagons of our defenses, and to make sure that we protect ourselves from another attack. Unfortunately, in doing so, we also cut ourselves off from the best source of genuine happiness. Now, I am not saying that bad or abusive relationships should be restored (although I believe not all in such categories are lost causes), but I am saying that the cynical nature that is often born when our hearts are broken robs us worse than the original transgression. We have no guarantees that we won't be hurt again, but we also have no guarantees that we will.

Many people in this world experience relationships as a source of deep pain and affliction. Spiritual storms of trouble and discontent swirl at the center of them. We find them in our workplaces, our play places, our homes, and even our churches. Such persons look like you and me, but they are often openly disagreeable, preferring, whether consciously or not, *trouble*making over *peace*making any day. But there are also those who seek health and restoration in relationships, and in whose presence such maladies as jealousy, bitterness, spitefulness, and duplicity cannot exist. These people are *peace*makers, and they are doing the work of God. Although too rare in this world, the *peace*makers provide the intimate connection back to God. They bridge the distance between how human nature wants to work and how God can work through us.

The seventh blessing is about the risky business of relationships and the important work that can make them stronger and better. Jesus knows that when we live faithfully in community, we do not necessarily reduce the risk of a broken heart, but we do raise the value of getting the journey right. Better yet, we live out the real point of our own creation, namely, to reflect God's image. Quite frankly, the world needs more *imago Dei*, more of Christ's reflection in our own, more relationships reflecting God's love and work for others to follow. No sight on earth is more peaceful, more uniting, or more like God.

Notes

1. Barbara Brown Taylor, *Home by Another Way* (Cambridge: Cowley Publications, 1999), 46.

2. Wendelin Van Draanen Parsons, *Flipped* (New York: Alfred A. Knopf, 2001).

3. William Barclay, *The Gospel of Matthew*, vol. 1 (Louisville: Westminster John Knox Press, 2001), 125-26.

4. Ibid.

5. Ibid., 126.

6. Ibid., 125.

7. *Phi Delta Kappan* 87, no. 4 (December 2005): 266-74.

8. Ibid., 266.

9. Ibid., 267-72.

10. Ibid., 264-65.

11. Ibid., 266.

The Eighth Blessing
The Tension of Choice

Rediscovering the Values of Jesus

*Blessed are those who are persecuted for righteousness'
sake, for theirs is the kingdom of heaven.*
—Matthew 5:10

*While I do not suggest that humanity will ever be able
to dispense with its martyrs, I cannot avoid the suspicion
that with a little more thought and a little less belief
their number may be substantially reduced.*
—J. B. S. Haldane[1]

Dispensing with Martyrs

I believe that J. B. S. Haldane is right—with less belief, we substantially reduce the number of martyrs. But that is real belief we are discussing. Today's church lacks the kind of fire and passion we saw from the early believers. Faithful belief births martyrdom; there is no way around it. The delicate balance of theology, God's presence with us, exists between authentic extremism and martyrdom, with too many of us living in between in some makeshift "holding area" for spiritual cowards. Certainly, I am not suggesting that martyrdom is a good thing. No one can read the lives of the early martyrs or even the present-day ones without a sense of sadness and dismay at humanity's ignorance.

The eighth blessing reminds us that in the tension of our choice between the things of God and the things of this world, we find glimpses of the Kingdom. This is more than just a blessing; it is the fulfillment of our greatest blessing, God's gift of faith and relationship in Jesus Christ. When we decide to throw down the gauntlet, commit, choose—however we want to characterize it—we take hold of our greatest gift and we find our hope. The joy of knowing God intimately, overcoming our grief, reaching beyond ourselves to help others, offering mercy, doing good, building right relationships—all of these values lead us to something deeper than ourselves, to something sweeter than we can imagine. We find our missing piece or incomparable center, and we take hold of it, breathe deeply, and rejoice.

Prime Numbers

I have never been very good at math. However, I appreciate the complex nature that the world of numbers offers. A few years ago, I joined a mathematician friend for lunch, and a strange conversation about prime numbers ensued. *Webster's* describes a *prime number* as a positive integer (>1) whose only divisors are itself and one. To be quite honest, I never wanted to know this. I have never been tempted to include prime numbers in a sermon illustration, newsletter article, or book chapter. In fact, the only reason the topic came up was a slip in my concentration. I had been focused not to mention math, realizing both my inability and my disinterest in where such a topic might lead. But she mentioned prime numbers. I blurted out, "So what is the deal with prime numbers? I mean it seems pretty ridiculous to be concerned with numbers that can only be divided by themselves."

I had never witnessed a mathematician become angry, but unlike any rumors you may have heard, the whole scene is visceral and dangerous. With a glassy look in her eyes, my friend spouted words like *Riemann hypothesis, Mersenne primes,* and *Drake's cryptogram,* and frighteningly, she was only beginning. I heard about *repeating integers, random supposition,* and *algorithms.* I concluded, mostly out of shame, that there is nothing ridiculous about prime numbers for mathematicians and, quite honestly, for the rest of us either.

Prime numbers serve as a code of sorts for all of humanity. While at first glance appearing without meaning, in reality, prime numbers are neither random nor disordered. Quite the opposite, they are mathematical building blocks for complex rationalities. And if this was not enough, in the middle of the conversation, I remembered that prime numbers are important for communicating with life forms from other worlds. If you read the book or saw the movie *Contact*, you understand. (To clarify for my fundamentalist friends, I am only joking.)

My friend continued discussing prime numbers in relation to the history of computer programming, medicine and, yes, theology. I sat stunned at the significance of what had seemed child's math, having had no idea of the genuine importance to both mathematics and the order of life. But nothing prepared me for her final comment. As she paused, sitting there with a wry, approving smile at having toyed with another unbeliever, she said, "And to think, it all begins with *1*. You can't understand any of this without understanding that." And then she added, "Isn't math wonderful!" As a pastor, I felt my heart go out to her at this point.

Whether it is counting pennies or understanding the nature of prime numbers, the number 1 rules human existence, and it is not accidental design. The value of 1 dominates the spiritual, physical, and communal landscape. The critical nature of simplicity, like the number 1, is not just singularity, but also placement, whether in a math formula or in life. We don't begin unless we begin with ol' uno. A complex math problem begins with one number, a great journey begins with one step, a romance with one glance, a changed life with one simple word or touch. The incredible potential and power of simplicity are unlimited.

Humans also operate within the tension of one choice at a time. The potential of one person to alter the human equation has, for centuries, dominated our spiritual, political, and social landscapes. "It only takes one . . . ," I have often heard, referring to the possibility that one person's choice for action can change the dynamics of a situation. Rosa Parks would be a wonderful example. No, she did not single-handedly usher in the civil rights movement; that was years in the making. But her actions on that Montgomery bus did catalyze a movement in that place and time that, in turn, catalyzed others throughout the South.

The potential of one person to make *one* choice for something new, bold, or downright unbelievable possesses exceptional power. Evil, injustice, and prejudice thrive in complex and confusing situations when people are caught stunned or apathetic to the moment. What the forces of darkness cannot factor or effectively counter is one voice, one choice, one life that stands against the tide and is willing to make the ultimate sacrifice.

The Eight Blessings

Personal, Cosmic Choices

The *Stars Wars* saga remains one of my favorite movie series of all time. Since 1977, when my grandfather took me to see George Lucas's first installment of Luke, Leia, and Darth Vader, I have been enthralled by each subsequent chapter of this unfolding drama. Sure, I enjoy the cutting edge technology (at least for its day) and filmmaking, along with its odd, but engaging characters and worlds. But the most intriguing element of *Star Wars* is the constant tension between good and evil, expressed in the ongoing struggle between the Rebels and the Empire.

However, the moral dilemma is not just corporate in nature, but also plays out in the very personal relationship of Anakin (Darth Vader) and his son, Luke. Luke represents the uncorrupted version of his father, unencumbered by the bitter and dark draw of the Empire. Luke comes of age in this struggle and fights against seemingly insurmountable odds in the name of freedom and justice. In the final episode, *Return of the Jedi*, he is willing to lay down his own life for his friends and cause. Ultimately, good prevails, and order is restored to the universe. But the victory is not won in some grand, cosmic battle.

No, the victory begins with Luke's willingness to die for what he believes, forcing his father (Vader) to also choose from the depths of his own soul. The Emperor's demise (if you will endure a bit more theologizing) comes not from an army but from a father who summons more good than the ever-present evil can control. The tension in Vader leads him to kill the Emperor. We now know the entire story of how this final conflict was shaped and designed. Funny how no one comes into this world evil but either succumbs to or resists its seduction. Even for the personification of evil (the Emperor and Vader), it was a matter of choice.

I believe this is how we would like to view the world. Of course, we are keenly aware of the trouble; we feel it and experience its effects daily. Deep down, we are not so naïve as to think that our world really can exist without evil, persecution, or trial, but we crave the redemption of circumstances and souls in the end. The problem is that order is only part of the solution. The universe's restoration to order in *Star Wars* ceases only the immediate crisis; it does not conclude humanity's tendency to repeat the possible choosing of bad paths. No matter what we may believe, *The Return of the Jedi* will never be the end of the saga. No amount of order ever will be. Possibly, then, our focus should be not on the restoration of order, but on the willingness to give one's life for something more, better, and deeper that ultimately might change the pattern or provide an alternative path with new possibilities.

The early church, or Jesus for that matter, did not regard order as the primary experience or focus of the church. No, the life of faith expressed itself in moments seemingly inconsequential to the rest of the known world. But as we read in Acts and learn from the writings of the early Christian fathers, the church found its voice in an age that included real martyrs and persecution. The faith formed around choices that included, no less, the giving of one's life. In Acts 6, for example, the story of Stephen, although it reads as a watershed in light of our modern understanding of church history, included in the moment one solitary account of one solitary life. I question whether Stephen was actually the "first" martyr of the faith, but I believe he was certainly the most significant of his generation because of the contrast between his willingness to die for his faith and Saul's willingness to kill for his. Saul, also known as Paul, refocused his zeal when he chose to follow Jesus after his experience on the road to Damascus.

And so through the Beatitudes, Jesus sat on this mountainside sharing these blessings with his followers, keenly aware of where such living would lead. He knew that each blessing, if the disciples truly lived it, pushed this band of followers further from the established norms of the world and created an ongoing tension of great proportion. "Blessed are you when people . . . persecute you" (Matthew 5:11). Notice that Jesus did not say *if;* he said *when.* He understood the coming storm. In less than forty years after Jesus uttered these words to his disciples, the Romans utterly destroyed the Temple in Jerusalem.

Following the Resurrection, the movement of the Way (Acts 24:14) experienced times of intense persecution from the religious and political leaders of the day. On many occasions, those watching this small band of followers were unsure whether the movement could survive such treatment. The list of atrocities rivaled any the human imagination could employ, including unspeakable deaths by wild animals and public burnings.

The presence of persecution and those martyrs, in early Christian history, witnessed to the commitment of early Christians and to their developing moral force. In a world where it was not uncommon to create gods to fit the worldview of one society to another, the Christian movement offered the importance of choice, establishing a firm connection to the Creator and a moral standard based upon God's ways of justice and mercy. The first seven blessings provide a clear connection to God and to one another, challenging every human discourse from self-sufficiency to poverty. Jesus knew that living as a Christian, especially under the guidance of these Blessings, created a way of life that challenged the political and religious establishment and that set human beings firmly against the spiritual and moral expectations of this world. Followers of God's way would not fit clearly within predefined patterns of existing religious and political structures. Certainly, the institutionalization of the church complicates this voice by reducing Christianity to another human endeavor, but the Blessings sit beyond any institutional experience, and when they are lived fully, even in our overtly Christian world, they create a distinction that is both obvious and uncomfortable. However, even the deepest, most profound parts of Christian doctrine begin with the formula of one heart and one choice.

Running to the Fire

And so, let's get real for a moment. What we are talking about is not easy; it is not comfortable to talk about persecution. It strains us to consider that faith has requirements that are more distinct than simply giving our time or resources to a particular congregation. No, real faith in Christ pushes us and causes us to think deeply about how we live our lives, how we treat others, and especially how we treat this God we claim to love so much. It is fanciful, if not downright delusional, to think that a God who can "throw stars around" is satisfied by our simply arriving in a comfortable building to "memorialize" God. Thankfully and graciously, there is more to faith than memorializing, and if we are to be called Christian, we must find what is more to life and live it.

As a little boy, I remember, like many little boys, wanting to be a fireman. There was something magical about putting on the gear, coat, and boots, donning the red hat, and jumping on the truck with sirens blaring.

Heading off to the blaze seemed exciting; an adventure that, to a child, had no bad endings or untimely deaths. No, in the end, the firemen put out any inferno, rescued people, and saved the day. Being a fireman meant all of the pizzazz without any of the danger or the dread. Thankfully for those who would have depended on me for their well-being, I was led to other vocational pursuits, and my dream of being a fireman never came to fruition.

I guess it is easy to fantasize about jobs, roles, or responsibilities that, we know, do not actually require any hardship or discomfort—and certainly no sacrifice. Don't get me wrong. I am glad that little boys and girls dream big dreams and play dress up complete with make-believe worlds. However, sooner or later, the fantasies stop, and we confront a very real world with real problems that demand real action and response. Too many times, the same little boys and girls who charge the hill in *make-believe* find themselves timid and unsure as adults, especially when it comes to living out what they really believe.

This especially hit home on September 11, 2001. Like so many others, I watched spellbound as the events unfolded on television. The first news report of a plane hitting the North Tower of the World Trade Center captivated our attention. Watching the *Today Show*, I was stunned when the second plane struck, exploding into the South Tower. At that moment, we knew our world had changed. Over the next hour or so, I sat in shock as people evacuated the burning buildings, ever mindful of the ones who would most certainly never leave. When the towers fell, the scene became almost surreal. I wanted the scene to be a disaster movie instead of reality. But unlike any disaster movie, this was no alien attack or major climate shift. This disaster came at the hands of faithful men from another faith, whose misguided doctrine caused them to end their lives along with thousands of others by flying into the heart of a skyscraper. News from an attack on the Pentagon along with an odd crash of another jet in a Pennsylvania hillside further disrupted our world's order. For many Americans, the questions engraved themselves deep into our souls as we watched commitment to religion play out in barbaric fashion. Why would men do *this* in the name of God? It was the first of many questions that day clawing for some sort of understanding of how this could happen. But deep down, another question also pierced my soul and, later I would discover, the souls of others. If these men would do this for their God, what would I do for mine? And in such an unbelievably twisted means as this, if these men would plunge themselves into the fiery blast of aircraft fuel to proclaim their devotion to a doctrine of death, what fire, if any, would I run to in order to proclaim my faith in the God of life?

One particular image of September 11 that will remain with me for the rest of my life is a still photo taken in a stairwell of the North Tower not long before the tower's collapse. While a long line of people heading down the stairs forms to the right, the photo shows two lone firemen making their way up the stairway on the left. The eyes of the lead fireman struck me as he looked directly into the camera. It is a haunting image of sheer terror laced with amazing courage. I do not know who took the photo or even where I remember seeing it, but I will never forget the image.

These two firemen, along with all of the first responders, did not have the luxury of make-believe worlds any longer. Their devotion to their vocations, to one another, and to complete strangers trumped any sense of adventure or excitement. As so many people made their way from the scene of the blast and the raging inferno, these people ran to the fire and, for many, to their deaths. But in the real world, that is what firemen do. While others move away, they are not only undeterred by the fire, but they are trained and expected to move toward it. For firemen, it is simply who they are called to be.

When it comes to our faith, I am afraid that we Christians have too often allowed ourselves to exist in some make-believe world where faith means being comfortable and being fed. Jesus never promised such for those who would follow him. No, Jesus' promise for his followers included crosses and troubled times, but also a victory that overcomes such obstacles. However, it is easier to convince ourselves that the Christian journey will be "roses and rituals" that lead only to safe places. But if we are to be honest and faithful, we know that this is *make-believe* and that our journey, although profound, beautiful, and meaningful, will require more than we are often willing to share. It will require places that stretch us, make us uncomfortable, and call from us those feelings, emotions, and actions that can be characterized only as courageous. And this journey will require that we run to the fire and be unafraid. We are Christians, followers of the Way. It is what we do. It is who we are called to be.

The Power of Choices

Jesus understood the power of choice. We see glimpses throughout his ministry of his incredible decision to be among us, to live incarnate within our frame. Paul discusses this in his letter to the Philippians as he shares the Christ Hymn and sings the praise and awe of God with us. His encouragement that we might become like Christ ultimately centers on the unbelievable, otherworldly choice that the Son of God made to "humble himself" in such a dramatic way. This choice, though taken for granted now, seemed incomprehensible in the general wave of religious thought in Jesus' day. Although the ancient stories showed that gods enjoyed being among human beings for one fancy or another, in general, human beings wanted to become gods; gods did not want to become human. The Incarnation is remarkable in that it sets the stage for the power of choices, and God, through Christ, provides an example of how God's choice for us changed not only our destiny but also the entire world.

The same exists for our choices today. Many times, the world pushes against our faith, challenging us at the deepest places. We choose God's ways, not because they are easy or comfortable, but because they serve as the doorway for how we live as Christ in our world. We do not experience the same types of choices as our brothers and sisters before us. For most of us, there are no actual lions ready to tear us to shreds or executioners poised to kill us. But the choices are still very real and sit starkly against their overall spiritual impact. And such choices for Christ do not bring easy paths or roads. In fact, as it was in the days of the early martyrs, it is still easier to choose the way of the world instead of following Christ. Whether our stage is a coliseum, a workplace, or a school yard, the screams still beckon, and the choices remain tough.

In making a choice, we delineate ourselves from the standards of the world and establish a genuine point of reference that marks our place in this great story of faith. As one pastor friend remarked, we become a living expression of Hebrews 11, continuing in fine fashion as the "next chapter" of God's unfolding narrative. Sure, it may be difficult to see ourselves aligned with the martyrs, especially in a world where Christianity has become the dominant institution, but every time we side with God's work and grace in our midst, something remarkable happens. For some, it is simply another example of God's presence within and among us. But for others, it is real choices in real places with real enemies and struggles. And it takes only one such encounter to define our moment for Christ.

That moment makes it all worthwhile, the belief, the sacrifice, and the hope that there is something deeper and better to it all. It is in the choosing between the ways of the world and the hope of our Savior that sets the tones of our souls forever. Some will say Christianity is a passive faith of old churches, pews, and fixtures. But Christianity is far from such. Regardless of how the church looks today, the faith itself still pushes the edges of our society, showing a better way and proclaiming a new day for captives, prisoners, rich, poor, marginalized, lost, found, and everyone in between. Real Christianity is far from passive; it is passionate, faithful, uncomfortable and, at times, dangerous. It is also the open doorway to God's kingdom, and we have been asked to make our way inside.

The eighth blessing is more than just the martyrs' or the persecuted's blessing. It is a reminder that in Christ's presence there are no spectators. For Christ himself said, "Whoever is not with me is against me" (Matthew 12:30 NRSV). There is power in the choosing. There is freedom in the choosing. There is grace in the choosing. There is example in the choosing. There is hope in the choosing. But we must choose.

Note

1. J. B. S. Haldane, "The Duty of Doubt," in *Possible Worlds and Other Essays* (London: Chatto & Windus, 1927).

AFTERWORD
ARE YOU PREPARED FOR A BLESSING?

The intermediate theological category between God and human fortune is, as far as I can see, that of blessing. . . . Indeed, the only difference between the Old and New Testaments in this respect is that in the Old the blessing includes the cross, and in the New the cross includes the blessing.
—Dietrich Bonhoeffer[1]

"Are you prepared for a blessing?" The question seemed odd, but at 1:30 a.m., "odd" was all that filled the airwaves. I am a notoriously bad sleeper and spend a significant amount of time watching late night television. My insomnia is a result of too many medicines and, I am convinced, an out-of-date mattress. Regardless, I have grown somewhat accustomed to visiting with my nocturnal friends by way of the tube.

A person who watches late night television should be prepared for a variety of interesting folks and entertainment, including just about every televangelist with a bad hairdo and prayer cloths. One of my favorites is a middle-aged Midwestern fellow with dyed hair and a misguided message of prosperity and healing. In fact, his reading of Scripture is so skewed that I often find myself, Bible opened, matching his various principles with my own proclamations of rebuttal. I knew the Bible drill program (circa second through fifth grades) would come in handy!

On this particular night, the topic was "how to receive a blessing by simply sending money to feed starving children." I figured he actually needed it to pay for airtime and the lease on a Lexus, but when he asked if I was prepared for a blessing, having spent a year with the Eight Blessings nailed to my wall and not averse to being blessed myself, my ears perked up. Brother Hairdo said that if I would send twenty-five dollars, I would receive a prayer cloth. Not only that, but if I would wipe my forehead with the prayer cloth and return it to him, he would pray over it and whatever ailed me would be healed. And if this offer was not good enough, I would also receive a financial blessing for my act of faith that would allow me, of course, to provide more opportunities for future blessings—sort of a spiritual pyramid program.

Although logic told me that this man would never pray over my prayer cloth, no matter how many times I wiped my forehead, and that my qualifications for a blessing have little to do with my checkbook, I still found myself intrigued by the offer. I believe all of us want to be blessed. We want the hurt to go away, the worries to subside, and the ache to let go. Although I shouted phrases like "fake" and "get a style consultant" at Brother Hairdo, I couldn't blame him for asking the question. Somewhere in the daily trudge of life, we have forgotten that not only has God been asking this question for millennia, but on a hill some two thousand years ago, God answered it through Jesus.

Most of us believe we understand what it means to be blessed. I have heard the phrase "what a blessing" countless times, usually expressing an otherwise unexplainable emotion or feeling. People talk about blessings in both personal and random terms. Some will say, "My children are such a blessing," or "This friendship is a real blessing." Certainly, there are infinite expressions of gratitude, love, and fortune enmeshed in such comments.

But others use *blessing* when other words cannot be found. "The stranger who helped me fix a flat on the side of the road was a true blessing," or "The extra fifty dollars I found stuck behind my dresser was an unexpected blessing." What we really mean by these statements is, "I am not sure what to make of these," or "I want to think that God sent the stranger or planted the cash for me to find, but people might find it odd." Either way, *blessing* is a safe choice.

A mom might say, "My children are a real blessing," when she actually means, "God gave them to me, and although they are driving me crazy, I have to love them anyway." Get the picture?

Blessing, like many words, loses its focus in our modern readings. It becomes a statement, opinion, presumption, or wish instead of a declarative appeal to the presence of God and sincere "thanks" for all that presence means. For Jesus, the Beatitudes do not exist as mere statements. He uses them as a means of exclamation to announce what each blessing means for those courageous souls who live faithfully according to the values they express. The Greek word used in Matthew 5 is *makarios*. An adjective, the word describes the joy of those who live and adhere faithfully to the values Jesus proclaims. He intends these words to transform a person's understanding of faith and the world. But Jesus' urgency in these statements propels the listener to joy, not despair. "What could our world be," Jesus inherently asks, "if we were to live in such a way?"

Makarios describes a "joyful" blessing that cannot be diminished by the ebb and flow of the world. Our English word *happiness* pales in properly explaining the possibilities of unadulterated, unobstructed joy that cannot be destroyed, no matter the circumstance. I like this word. It speaks to my own circumstances and to that feeling I get when I can't explain how I, a legally blind hemophiliac with HIV and hepatitis C, still believe God is good and gracious, and that each day seems a gift of twenty-four hours. No, the word *happiness* just doesn't cover it—I have been down that road, only to have one blood test or another quell my joy. A falling T-cell count does not make you feel blessed if your marker is the world's standard of happiness. On the other hand, *makarios* works just fine for me.

Many recoil at this kind of joy as a form of fancy or wishful thinking. "Marx was right," one atheist friend announced. "Religion is just a drug." But my response is always the same—I don't want to serve a God who looks at the condition of my body, state of mind, or wayward soul to predict the possibilities of my life. No, I want a God who says, "Pay no attention to the world's standards. This is the way to find real joy." As Jesus began to teach the disciples, these exclamations of blessing did just that.

Unveiling the Better Parts of Our Souls

Several weeks ago, I wrote a column focusing on the importance of being financially prepared for the unknown. At the time, I taught stewardship for the United Methodist Foundation. I used an illustration, shared by a friend who lived through Hurricane Camille, about the power of catastrophic events to alter and inform our futures. As I wrote in the article, "most people will never endure such a catastrophic event as Camille, but as my friend has said many times, it only takes *one* to change your life forever." How ironic.

These same friends rode out Hurricane Katrina in my home and lived with us for the next eight days. No one could have imagined the ferocious nature of this monster storm, including these veterans of Camille.

We watched for hours as the winds and rain battered our neighborhood, toppling large trees. Thankfully, the largest and last of our pine trees came to rest diagonally away from our home.

When the fiercest part of the storm passed, my friend, an employee of a local utility company, headed out to survey the damage. As we literally cut our way out of the subdivision, we could not believe what we discovered—impassable roads, destroyed power lines, heavily damaged buildings and property. So much destruction, especially for a town that sits nearly seventy-five miles from the Gulf Coast.

When we returned home, my friend's company radio reached fellow workers stranded in Gulfport. The reports were horrific. Entire city blocks were leveled. Places that had weathered every major hurricane on the coast in the past 150 years were gone. One colleague's comment said it all: "This made Camille look like a summer shower."

Later, we learned that our friends' family members were safe but their homes completely destroyed. Even homes built to "Camille standards," complete with all of the hurricane-proofing materials, were nothing more than concrete slabs. The conversation between my friend and his brother was especially poignant.

"You mean the houses are gutted?" my friend asked.

"No, Jeff," his brother replied. "I mean they are gone; they are just not there."

The word *gone* now has a new and more profound meaning.

Katrina's storm did not end with the subsiding of winds. Over the next days, we watched as one community after another confronted issues that are unthinkable in our modern American society, including the very real potential of panic and civil unrest. I could not fathom military police directing traffic in our small hometown as hundreds of people lined up for the basic necessities of food and water.

Aside from the horrific scenes of New Orleans, other communities, less accustomed to humanity's darker side, found themselves pushing back against fear, panic, and loss. Rumors, prejudice, and stereotypes flourished in these days of incredible uncertainty. For many, the conversations dealt less with recovery and rebuilding and more with simply evacuating a disturbing scene.

At first glance, it appeared that Katrina brought only the worst of nature's fury and the worst of human suffering. But as happens with the dawn of each day, people found glimpses of new light in the rubble of broken homes, landscapes, and lives. The stories of whole communities joining for meals and care echoed the account in Acts of the first-century church as believers trusted each other for support and encouragement (Acts 2:42-47).

After the worst week of most people's lives, Sunday came, and Christians met for worship on empty lots, formerly the sites of their sanctuaries. Churches from around the world sent supplies and teams to respond, many times long before any official authority arrived. In my hometown, a local Baptist congregation served hot meals three times a day while other congregations dispersed ice, water, and clothes.

As rumors of unspeakable tragedy unfolded, so did talk of incredible acts of random kindness—strangers giving their time to assist those who had been unable to prepare for the storm's onslaught. Word came as neighbors, who had only days before been merely passing acquaintances, were welcomed into one another's homes.

Our local church organized family kits of food, water, and baby supplies to be distributed in hard-hit rural areas. People did not complain about leaving their own homes to distribute supplies. We felt privileged for the opportunity to do something—anything! When my family dropped off food at a local apartment complex of young, underresourced families, I found myself thanking *them* for allowing me to respond to their need, for as I responded to their need, my own emptiness was filled.

Maybe Katrina did not just bring the worst. Maybe in the wake of such a natural tragic catastrophe we saw the better part of our souls. Maybe in the shadows of our vulnerability, we became available to reach beyond our self-interests and divisions.

Certainly, Katrina highlighted the worst people can experience, but she also unveiled some of the best. She revealed the interdependence we ultimately have with one another.

A friend repeated a conversation his grandchildren had two days after the storm while they were gathering debris in his yard. With no electricity, local children found themselves away from television and computers and outside playing through the neighborhood. Several had stopped by to assist with cleaning.

My friend's ten-year-old grandson, frustrated that the "helping hands" of neighbors' kids were not "cleaning" the way he wanted, complained about their lack of order and direction.

His seven-year-old sister responded by saying, "Stop being a big, stinking crybaby! You know we can't do this without them."

How true! Whether it is the debris in the front yard or in the recesses of our lives—we just cannot clean it up alone.

Disaster reminds us of things that we would rather forget—fragile lives, death, despair, destruction. However, it also has the potential to show us the better parts of the journey—authentic friendships, real compassion, and genuine heroes.

After several days of being without electricity and having to carry water from my fountain to flush the toilets, I became more of a "big, stinking crybaby" than I am proud to admit. But we must now help those who have lost so much face a future that will require great patience, commitment, and perseverance. As Acts 2 people, we have confronted such trials before, and thankfully, graciously, God never intends for us to face them alone.

The Real Blessing

The nature of real "blessing" is in knowing that God never leaves and that God brings God's people together. God shows us a beautiful, indispensable resource in serving each other. When we care deeply about our brother or sister, we discover comfort for our beleaguered souls. We do not care about others' or God's standards out of selfish expectation or in the desire to be blessed. We care because Jesus taught us to care about others, about how they feel, live, and die. Jesus taught us to care about those we love, but even more about those we don't love, for such caring is the mark of a true follower of the Way. Jesus taught us to care because in doing the seemingly irresponsible, irrational things of the world, like *turning the other cheek, loving your enemies, and giving yourself away for nothing in return*, we find our lives, and life is all the sweeter. Many times, I don't want to care—it is easier and more expedient to, once again, retreat to those corners and be ready to fight. However, the Beatitudes in Matthew 5 show us a better way.

The most important question in the Eight Blessings for Christians is to genuinely ask what makes Jesus' message different. The answer is that in setting a new spiritual and moral standard for the world, Jesus embraced people—blemishes and all—with real-world values that bind us together rather than divide us. No encounter with Jesus in the Gospels leaves us without the distinct impression that all of us fit somewhere in the story—some as Pharisees, some as faithful, some as saints, and some as sinners. Jesus welcomes all of us, not because we deserve it or because we are right, but because God through Christ has so loved *the world*.

To the chagrin of many, heaven will look a lot like the world, only redeemed, settled, and less angry. But Jesus is clear that the kingdom of God, as found on that day, begins here and now, and whether we like or not, we have been called to proclaim it and live like we belong there. And *that* is a blessing!

I could never understand why my grandmother could cling to such hope in God even when her hope for life faded. But after seeing the Blessings come to life, I now know. She saw beyond the natural impediments. My grandmother did not see faith in Christ as a litany of to do's or tasks that kept her in good graces with the Creator. She felt genuine relationship with God, and while I was busy trying to make sense of it all, she touched the face of God and found entrance to the Kingdom. To her, the cancer was not persecution; it was just life's last grasp at keeping her from seeing what it had all meant from the beginning—the last, momentary prick before unspeakable joy. The Blessings sat by her bed to remind her that this was, indeed, not the end, but merely the beginning for all of us who believe. Her words became truer to me time and again through each of the Beatitudes. In these truths taught and lived by Jesus, we are most certainly blessed.

Note

1. Dietrich Bonhoeffer, *Letters and Papers from Prison* (New York: Macmillan, 1953), 347.

STUDY GUIDE

This study guide provides additional focus for individuals and small groups interested in developing their understanding of the Beatitudes. Written to encourage dialogue and reflection, each section is divided into four parts.

The first part, *Reveal*, allows for a deeper unveiling of the scripture text. Although certainly not exhaustive in nature, the questions provide a starting point for further discussion. The second part, *Reflect*, addresses more personal questions derived from themes of the texts by encouraging readers to think diligently about how the text affects, instructs, and ignites their particular perspective on the topic. The third section, *Respond*, enlists the readers to transform words into action by responding to the Beatitudes in tangible ways that can have an effect on their world. The last section, *Refine*, takes the reader deeper into scripture and self-discovery by addressing various supplemental texts and principles related to the Beatitudes. The section also leads the reader deeper into the Sermon on the Mount and encourages the application of the Beatitudes in relation to the various topics and issues Jesus raises.

The purpose of these questions is to immerse seekers and believers into the life of God as presented by Jesus in the Beatitudes.

THE FIRST BLESSING

Having Nothing, Possessing Everything

Blessed are the poor in spirit, for theirs is the kingdom of heaven.
—Matthew 5:3

Read Matthew 5:3; Psalms 34:1-10; 68:7-10; 72:2-4; and 132:13-18. Read the chapter titled "The First Blessing: Having Nothing; Possessing Everything."

REVEAL

• In what ways do Jennifer's and Mark's "limitations" allow them to draw closer to the heart of God?

• How does God use our struggles and "spiritual poverty" to help us see God's deeper work and will for our lives?

REFLECT

Jesus says we are **blessed when we empty ourselves so completely that only God remains.** *Emptying* ourselves requires putting aside old hurts, anger, and ambitions that keep us from seeing the presence of God. Why is this process so difficult, and what obstacles prevent us from *cultivating a healthy poverty* in order to see the work and will of God in our lives?

RESPOND

In what ways do you need to empty your life in order to see the work and will of God? Make a list of those attitudes, ambitions, and desires that keep us *spiritual debtors* to self. In what way can you specifically give those debts over to God and find true *spiritual riches*?

REFINE

Using a Bible commentary and dictionary, examine the following biblical themes and passages:

• Discover the view of the word *poor* in the Psalms. Describe God's special relationship, as told from the point of view of the psalmist, with those in need and utterly dependent.

• Move ahead in the Sermon on the Mount (Matthew 5–7). How does cultivating a *healthy poverty* for God change the way we pray or live out spiritual disciplines? How does cultivating a *healthy poverty* for God change the way we interact and care for one another? Finally, how does cultivating a *healthy poverty* for God alter the way we care for ourselves?

THE SECOND BLESSING

Joy Learned Only from Sorrow

Blessed are those who mourn, for they will be comforted.
—Matthew 5:4

Read Matthew 5:4 and Romans 8:31-39. Read the chapter titled "The Second Blessing: Joy Learned Only from Sorrow."

REVEAL

• As Abraham Verghese's quote states, how do our secrets create a spiritual sickness in our lives?

• In the lives of Tom and the gentleman who planted the tree in memory of his son, how does mourning help reveal the sweetness of relationship in our lives?

REFLECT

Jesus says we are **blessed when we have loved and lived to the point of great vulnerability and brokenness for, in such, we will find real joy and comfort in the heart of God.** *Real love* requires great risk and a fragile approach to life. Why do great love and the risk of great mourning go hand in hand? Describe a *risk-free* life.

RESPOND

In what ways do you *mourn* today? Make a list of regrets, obstacles, and losses that fill your heart and life with mourning. In what ways can you specifically give your grief and brokenness to God and restore your joy and comfort? In what ways can you help relieve the brokenness and mourning of others? How can we change actions that bring sorrow and grief to the world?

REFINE

Using a Bible commentary and dictionary, examine the following biblical themes and passages:

• Discover the view of the word *mourning* in the Old Testament. In Genesis 37, Jacob believes his son Joseph is dead. In verse 34, describe Jacob's grief at the loss of his son.

• In Matthew 9 and John 16, Jesus teaches his disciples about God's comfort in the midst of great suffering. What is the focus of the disciples' grief in this passage? How does Jesus answer what will be their time of great mourning?

• Move ahead in the Sermon on the Mount (Matthew 5–7). How does cultivating a *broken life* for God change our approach to ethical or justice issues? How does cultivating a *broken life* for God change the way we interact and care for one another (for example, marriage)? Finally, how does cultivating a *broken life* for God alter the way we care for ourselves?

THE THIRD BLESSING

The Balanced Life

Blessed are the meek, for they will inherit the earth.
—Matthew 5:5

Read Matthew 5:5. Read the chapter titled "The Third Blessing: The Balanced Life."

REVEAL

• If you could write your obituary, what would it say? In what ways would you call your life "significant"?

• Reflecting on Lonny's story, what significant steps do you take in order to live a more "balanced life"?

REFLECT

Jesus says we are **blessed when we find God's balance between abundant and deficient in our lives.** *The spiritually balanced life* requires a focus on meaning and relationship while reducing selfishness and pride. Why is it oftentimes easier to follow our self-centered desires than to trust the work of God in our lives? How does the example of Jesus' earthly life and ministry inform how we should live *meekly* in the world?

RESPOND

Commit to a week of journaling in which you measure and reflect upon your decisions, looking specifically at decisions related to your spiritual walk with God and your relationship with others. Try using two columns, one for decisions that provide for spiritual balance and development, and a second for decisions that promote a more self-centered approach. Describe the impact or potential impact of those decisions.

REFINE

Using a Bible commentary and dictionary, examine the following biblical themes and passages:

• Read Proverbs 16:32. Why does the writer believe *patience* and *self-control* are keys to real significance in this world? How have you experienced these characteristics in your own life? What are their effects?

• Move ahead in the Sermon on the Mount (Matthew 5–7). How does cultivating a *balanced life* for God change the way we pray or live out spiritual disciplines? How does cultivating a *balanced life* for God change the way we interact and care for one another? Finally, how does cultivating a *balanced life* for God alter the way we care for ourselves?

THE FOURTH BLESSING

The Heart That Craves for God

Blessed are those who hunger and thirst for righteousness,
for they will be filled.
—*Matthew 5:6*

Read Matthew 5:6. Read the chapter titled "The Fourth Blessing: The Heart That Craves for God."

REVEAL

• Reflecting on Sam and Gayle's story, how can what we "crave" in this world affect our relationships, lives, and futures?
• What do you think happened to Sam and Gayle?
• Reflecting on the story of the woman and her mission team, how does what we crave affect our potential for living and doing the will of God in our world?

REFLECT

Jesus says we are **blessed when we crave complete righteousness and goodness as a starving person craves food or a thirsty person craves water.** Such craving requires an inexhaustible yearning for the work and presence of God in our lives. However, why does this process oftentimes become confused by other cravings in our lives? Describe the difference between *cravings of the world* and craving for God.

RESPOND

Make a list of those cravings in your life that run contrary to God's work in you. How can you specifically give those cravings to God? Make a list of ways we can *crave* after goodness and righteousness in our world.

REFINE

Using a Bible commentary and dictionary, examine the following biblical themes and passages:

• Read Matthew 6:33. Define the following terms: *seek, first, kingdom of God, all things.* How does a biblical understanding of these terms affect the meaning of Matthew 5:6 for you? What does God want from us as we seek God's will? What is the benefit of such seeking?

• Move ahead in the Sermon on the Mount (Matthew 5–7). How does cultivating *healthy cravings* for God change the way we pray or live out spiritual disciplines? How does cultivating *healthy cravings* for God change the way we interact and care for one another? Finally, how does cultivating *healthy cravings* for God alter the way we care for ourselves?

THE FIFTH BLESSING

Doing Life Together

Blessed are the merciful, for they will receive mercy.
—Matthew 5:7

Read Matthew 5:7; 6:9-15; Luke 11:2-4; Hebrews 2:17; Amos 5:23-24; and John 3:16-17; Matthew 19:14-15. Read the chapter titled "The Fifth Blessing: Doing Life Together."

REVEAL

• Reflecting on Elizabeth's and Maxine's story, how does seeing from only one point of view affect our understanding of God's work in our lives and the world?

• Reflecting on how communities have changed in the last generations, how do our home lives, schedules, and priorities affect the way we do life together?

REFLECT

Jesus says we are **blessed when we put ourselves in others' shoes and experience life as they do, for in such we will find understanding for our lives.** Experiencing the world from another's perspective requires a deliberate effort of self-denial in our lives. However, most will never *slow down their self-interests* long enough to see the world from another's perspective. Why? What are the benefits of walking in someone else's shoes and experience? What happens in relationships and circumstances when we refuse to do so?

RESPOND

Make a list of those on whom you have passed judgment without seeing their perspective. First, prayerfully consider their point of view. Make a list of what you might have missed from seeing things only from your vantage point. Second, take time to reconnect with those individuals as a deliberate effort of authentic *mercy* living.

REFINE

Using a Bible commentary and dictionary, examine the following biblical themes and passages:

• Read Hebrews 2:1-18. Describe the importance of Jesus' becoming human in order to be our perfect leader, priest, and Savior. Why does God's mercy in Christ require Jesus "stepping into our shoes"? Does the "taking away of our sins" (v. 17) include healing our separation from one another's perspectives?

• Move ahead in the Sermon on the Mount (Matthew 5–7). How does cultivating *authentic mercy living* for God change the way we pray or live out spiritual disciplines? How does cultivating *authentic mercy living* for God change the way we interact and care for one another? Finally, how does cultivating *authentic mercy living* for God alter the way we care for ourselves?

THE SIXTH BLESSING

Seeing Only What We Are Able to See

Blessed are the pure in heart, for they will see God.
—*Matthew 5:8*

Read Matthew 5:8; Proverbs 23:7-8; Matthew 23:25-26; 19:14; James 4:8. Read the chapter titled "The Sixth Blessing: Seeing Only What We Are *Able* to See."

REVEAL

• Reflecting on the section titled "A Beary Serious Promise," write a "life promise" to God. Now, write a similar promise to a significant relationship in your life.

• If an artist were to look at your life's "painting," would it be described as "dot to dot" or a masterpiece in process?

REFLECT

Jesus says we are **blessed when our motives, desires, lives, and expectations are focused on God.** What do you consider your most important desires or expectations for your life? Do these desires or expectations *fit* with God's work in the world? How would reshaping your desires or motives, thinking more about *why* you do something instead of just *doing* it, affect your relationship with God and with others?

RESPOND

Make a list of your last five major decisions. Did you make those decisions based on God's principles or on more self-centered principles? Would taking time to reflect on the reason for those decisions have made a difference in the outcome? Are there decisions in your life that need rethinking or re-forming in order to provide a healthier life? For what decisions in your life do you need to take time for celebration?

REFINE

Using a Bible commentary and dictionary, examine the following biblical themes and passages:

• Read 1 Corinthians 15:58. Describe the importance of Paul's encouragement for us to remain "strong and steady, always enthusiastic" (NLT) in God's work. How do these qualities influence our spiritual walk with God? How do these qualities lived out (or not) in our lives influence how others see God through us?

• Move ahead in the Sermon on the Mount (Matthew 5–7). How does cultivating *a pure heart* for God change the way we pray or live out spiritual disciplines? How does cultivating *a pure heart* for God change the way we interact and care for one another? Finally, how does cultivating *a pure heart* for God alter the way we care for ourselves?

THE SEVENTH BLESSING

Producing Right *Relationships*

Blessed are the peacemakers, for they will be called children of God.
—Matthew 5:9

Read Matthew 5:9. Read the chapter titled "The Seventh Blessing: Producing *Right* Relationships."

REVEAL

• Reflecting on Kozol's argument and observations, in what ways have you allowed your world to become ordered but without real meaning?

• Would you describe yourself as a peace "maker" or simply a peace "lover"?

REFLECT

Jesus says we are **blessed when we foster and develop right relationships.** Name your life's most important and enduring relationships. What circumstances or qualities make them so? What "work" do you provide in keeping these relationships healthy and whole? What causes these relationships to be weakened or unhealthy? How would the same focus on other relationships help develop or deepen them?

RESPOND

Make a list of relationships in your life that need healing. What were the primary causes behind the wounds and scars of these relationships? In what ways can you be responsible for providing a "healing framework" for making right those relationships? What stands as the greatest impediment to healing in these relationships? Now, thinking about other relationships, how can you nurture and care for these relationships to prevent wounds and unhealthy developments?

REFINE

Using a Bible commentary and dictionary, examine the following biblical themes and passages:

• Read Romans 15:1-7 (NLT). Describe the importance of Paul's encouragement for us to "be considerate of the doubts and fears" of others. What is Paul asking from us in being "patient and encouraging" with others as we wait for "God's promises"? How do these qualities influence the health of our relationships? How do these qualities lived out (or not) in our lives help us to be "peacemakers" for God?

• Move ahead in the Sermon on the Mount (Matthew 5–7). How does cultivating *right relationships* for God change the way we pray or live out spiritual disciplines? How does cultivating *right relationships* for God change the way we interact and care for one another? Finally, how do cultivating *right relationships* for God alter the way we care for ourselves?

THE EIGHTH BLESSING

The Tension of Choice

Blessed are those who are persecuted for righteousness' sake,
for theirs is the kingdom of heaven.
—Matthew 5:10

Read Matthew 5:10; Acts 6; Matthew 5:11; Acts 24:14. Read the chapter titled "The Eighth Blessing: The Tension of Choice."

REVEAL

• Reflecting on the section titled "Running to the Fire," in what ways do you "run to the fire" for your faith?

• Why do you believe God gives *us* the choice as to whether we boldly respond or not respond to God's work in our lives?

REFLECT

Jesus says we are **blessed when we are persecuted for making a choice for him.** Why does choosing to follow Christ bring such pushback from the world? In what ways have you been called to make a choice for Christ? What were the results of your choice? Did this choice require you to take a stand against the standards of the world or to confront an issue? How do "everyday" choices influence our faith? Do our daily lives make "choices" even when we are not conscious of them? Describe.

RESPOND

Make a list of habits or lifestyles that do not reflect the love and example of Christ. Make a list of habits or lifestyles that "sit out" living for Christ in the world, maybe not by their antagonism, but by their lack of choosing for him. What actions can you take that will provide a "clear choice" for Christ in your world?

REFINE

Using a Bible commentary and dictionary, examine the following biblical themes and passages:

• Read Philippians 2:1-11. Discuss Paul's description of Christ's example in becoming like us. How does this "choice" by Christ in the Incarnation provide an example of what God asks us to choose in Jesus? Describe the characteristics outlined by Paul. In what ways can we follow Christ's example in choosing to be like him? How might such a choice bring discomfort or even persecution by the world?

• Move ahead in the Sermon on the Mount (Matthew 5–7). How does cultivating *a choice* for God change the way we pray or live out spiritual disciplines? How does cultivating *a choice* for God change the way we interact and care for one another? Finally, how does cultivating *a choice* for God alter the way we care for ourselves?